MARCO POLO'S PRECURSORS

MARCO POLO'S PRECURSORS

BY

LEONARDO OLSCHKI

With a map of Asia

1972

OCTAGON BOOKS

New York

Reprinted 1972
by special arrangement with The Johns Hopkins Press

OCTAGON BOOKS
A DIVISION OF FARRAR, STRAUS & GIROUX, INC.
19 Union Square West
New York, N. Y. 10003

LIBRARY OF CONGRESS CATALOG CARD NUMBER: 73-159218

ISBN 0-374-96146-8

Printed in U.S.A. by
NOBLE OFFSET PRINTERS, INC.
NEW YORK 3, N. Y.

TO

SAMUEL ELIOT MORISON

FOREWORD

This little book represents simultaneously the outline and condensation of a course of lectures delivered by the author in the Historical Seminar of the Johns Hopkins University during the academic year 1939/1940. It tries to explain the particular circumstances which made possible and successful the first systematic explorations of Central and Eastern Asia by the missionaries and merchants of the thirteenth century. The evolution of the first contacts between mediaeval Europe and Asia Major is considered here through the coordination and interpretation of the essential spiritual and cultural aspects of the enterprises which led to the discovery of the Far East by mediaeval travellers and to Marco Polo's *Description of the World*.

The principal objective of this essay is not the discussion of geographical and historical details nor a survey of well known travel accounts. This brief narrative of the early relations between the Western and Eastern worlds is chiefly intended as a description of the intellectual conquest of Asia by the travellers who transformed into an empirical reality the fabulous image of that continent created by poetry and fiction and confirmed by a tenacious traditional erudition. This is not a story of adventures but the critical interpretation of a human experience comparable only to the discovery of America. The similarity of the spiritual background connects this event with the objectives and experiences of the early explorers of Asia.

CONTENTS

MARCO POLO'S PRECURSORS

I. THE LITERARY PRECURSORS

Until about the middle of the thirteenth century, when the first missionaries set out " ad Tartaros," there prevailed in the Western world a profound and persistent ignorance of Central and Eastern Asia, an ignorance partially mitigated by a few vague and generic notions in which remote reminiscences of distant places and peoples were mingled with old poetic and mythical fables.[1] The Tartar invasion of Eastern and Central Europe in 1241 did not alter or even correct the conventional image of Asia popularized by poems and legends.[2] On the contrary, this bloody and destructive clash of the Mongolian and the Christian worlds left the latter just as ignorant of the physical and human aspects of Central and Eastern Asia as these Oriental peoples were of European civilisation.[2] No actual experience of warriors, travellers and traders contributed to the clarication of geographical and ethnological details concerning those regions known only by persistent erudite and literary traditions. At that time even such bookish and superficial knowledge of the interior of Asia was confined to the limits of the world known to the ancients. The

[1] An exposition of the mediaeval knowledge and ideas about Asia is set forth by John Kirtland Wright in *The Geographical Lore of the Time of the Crusades*, New York, 1925. What was known of eastern Asia is to be found in Henry Yule's *Cathay and the Way Thither*, new edition by H. Cordier, 4 vols., London, Hakluyt Society, 1915, especially Vol. I. A valuable anthology of pre-Columbian geographical authors and documents is R. Hennig's *Terrae Incognitae*, 4 vols., Leiden, 1936-39, with a verbose rather than ample commentary, and full bibliography.

[2] The Chinese knowledge of the West is recorded by Yule-Cordier, *Cathay*, etc., I, pp. 35-57 and by A. C. Moule, *Christians in China before the Year 1550*, London, 1930. Selections of translated Chinese texts on this subject in R. Hennig's *Terrae Incognitae*, Vol. I-III.

1

territories lying beyond the Caspian Sea, the Oxus, the Indus and the Ganges still appeared as the land of the Seres (the people referred to by Pliny), or as the Biblical kingdoms of the Magi and of Gog and Magog.[3] Commercial exchange contributed but little towards a practical knowledge of so many lands known only by more or less fantastic names. Recent studies and discoveries have proved, for example, that during the Middle Ages Chinese textiles found their way westwards where the technique of their manufacture and their ornamental designs spread throughout the Moslem and Christian worlds.[4] Merchants journeyed over the

[3] The legend of Gog and Magog (first studied by A. Graf in the Appendix to his *Roma nella Memoria e nelle Immaginazioni del Medio Evo*, Torino, 1893. Vol. II, p. 507 *et seq.*) refers, in part, to the regions bordering on China and the Great Wall of which probably something was known in Central and Western Asia, both among the Mongolians, against whom it was built, and among the Moslems, some of whom had penetrated as far as those regions in different epochs (cf. Yule-Cordier, *Cathay*, etc., I, pp. 83 *et seq.* and 124 *et seq.*). In Europe, however, Gog and Magog were localized in the " Caucasus " (cf. A. Graf, *op. cit.*, p. 557) which means in ancient and mediaeval geography the Hindu Kush, Pamir and Himalaya and the vaguely known mountain ranges of Central Asia (J. K. Wright, *passim*). Marco Polo, perhaps under Moslem influence, identifies the region of Gog and Magog with the land of Tenduc, a territory which, according to him, had formerly belonged to Prester John and was situated beyond the eastern limits of the Desert of Gobi and within the northern bend of the Yellow River (cf. *The Book of Ser Marco Polo* etc., transl. and edit. by Sir Henry Yule, 2 vols., 3rd ed., London, 1921, *passim*). The legend of Gog and Magog like that of Alexander the Great, undoubtedly owes its popularity in the Christian world to the fact that it is mentioned in the Sacred Scriptures and references to it in the *Koran* without doubt contributed to its diffusion in the Mohammedan world (cf. respective articles in the *Encyclopaedia of Island*, London, 1913, and the same passages quoted by R. Hennig, *op. cit.*, II, p. 185 *et seq.*). Besides, this same legend forms a part of the cycle of Alexander the Great in which all the mediaeval fables of Asia find their outlet. Cf. Andrew R. Anderson, *Alexander's Gate, Gog and Magog, and the Inclosed Nations*, Cambridge, Mass., 1932.

[4] On the commercial exchanges between Central and Eastern Asia and the West new light has been thrown by the excavations, discoveries and

same two routes used by the traders of Roman times: either across the China seas, India, the Persian Gulf, and Mesopotamia, or else by the continental routes to Persia through the desert of Gobi and Sinkiang, over the Pamir passes and through Western Turkestan.[5] This commercial intercourse, however, was always indirect and was brought about by intermediaries of diverse origin who spoke many different languages. Hence it would be a mistake to suppose—what has indeed been widely accepted as a fact—that exchange of goods implied also an exchange of culture. In this respect, the only detailed information handed down by the ancient world regarding the far East and its inhabitants is most instructive.[6] It passed unaltered from the books

studies of Sir A. Stein, especially in his works *Ancient Khotan*, Oxford, 1907; *On Ancient Central Asian Tracks*, London, 1933; and *Innermost Asia*, 1928. For the ancient geographical lore, cf. N. Cary and H. Warmington, *The Ancient Explorers*, London, 1929, pp. 56-85 and 130-164.

[5] The commercial Asiatic routes of antiquity are described, and their records annotated by M. B. Charlesworth, *The Trade Routes of the Roman Empire*, 2nd edit., Cambridge, 1924, p. 57 et seq. and p. 97 et seq. For the commercial exchanges of the Middle Ages, cf. the still basic works of W. Von Heyd, *Histoire du Commerce du Levant au Moyen Age*, Leipzig, 1886. A short survey with notes and map in the essay of Eileen Power, "Routes to Cathay," *Travel and Travellers of the Middle Ages*, edit. by A. P. Newton, New York, 1930, pp. 124-158. A new and daring view upon real and supposed relations between events in Asia and Europe is advanced by Frederick J. Teggart, *Rome and China*, Berkeley, Calif., 1939, reviewed by C. M. Wilbur in *Amer. Hist. Rev.*, Vol. XLVI, 1940, p. 93 et seq. *China and the West*, of W. E. Soothill, Oxford, 1925 and L. R. Hughes's, *The Invasion of China by the Western World*, London, 1937, offer but little to the subject of our particular interest. G. F. Hudson's *Europe and China*, London, 1925 contains an excellent survey of the trends and events in the evolution of those intercontinental relations. A modern interpretation from the economic, sociological and geo-political angles is given by Owen Lattimore in *Inner Asian Frontiers of China*, New York, 1940.

[6] Cf. the extracts from Greek and Latin authors collected by Yule-Cordier, *Cathay*, etc., p. 183 et seq. The latest study of ancient imaginative views about the Far East by A. Hermann, *Das Land der Seide*

of Pliny and Ammianus Marcellinus into mediaeval texts in the vulgar tongue intended for the laity. These texts represent the geographical conceptions of traders, travellers and sailors or of the public at large much better than the contemporary Latin literature of an erudite character.[7] A typical work of this kind is the famous *Trésor* written in France by the Florentine scholar and diplomat, Brunetto Latini.

In accord with the Latin authors mentioned above, he relates that " beyond the immense solitudes and uninhabited lands of the East . . . beyond all the dwellings of men, are a people called Scir or Seres, who, from leaves and the bark of trees which they subject to the action of water, make for themselves a woolen material with which they clothe their bodies. These people are peaceful and live amicably together among themselves, refusing the company of other peoples." " But our traders," continues the narrative, " pass over one of their rivers, where, on its further shores, they find all manner of merchandise. Without speaking, they examine the merchandise and decide by looking at it the price of each piece. And when they have seen it they take away what they wish, leaving in the place of each article its equivalent value. In this wise the natives sell their wares, neither do they desire little or much of ours." [9]

und Tibet im Lichte der Antike, Leipzig, 1939, utilizes the earlier literature on the subject and tries to connect, more or less successfully, the fantastic data offered by classical authors with the supposed geographical and ethnographical reality of prehistoric times.

[7] Cf. Charles V. Langlois, *La Connaissance de la Nature et du Monde au Moyen Age d'après les Ecrits français à l'usage des Laïcs*, Paris, 1927.

[8] *Livre dou Tresor*, written between 1262 and 1266, published by R. Chabaille, Paris, 1863.

[9] *Ed. cit.*, p. 158. This passage of the *Trésor* has been overlooked by Yule-Cordier, who quote, however, the sources of Latini's report (*Cathay,*

This narrative is significant as it accounts, in a form more symbolic than actual, for the mystery which shrouded the origin of such precious merchandise, despite centuries of commercial intercourse and some political and religious contacts with the contemporary rulers of Central and Eastern Asia.[10] It shows us through the story of mute exchanges how the acquisition of exotic goods did not at all imply an attainment of geographical knowledge or a broadening of cultural horizons. The Romans of the Imperial epoch imported silk at the price of its weight in gold but they had no exact idea of its origin or method of manufacture. Silk was considered to be a vegetable substance obtained, like linen or hemp, through a process of soaking in water or, as Vergil (*Georgics*, II, 121) and Pliny (*Hist. Natur.*, VI, 54) affirmed, a species of finest vegetable wool found hanging on trees which the Seres combed and gathered.[11]

etc., p. 196 *et seq.* and p. 203). The peculiarity of mute commercial exchanges, described by ancient geographers, is to be found also in Vulgar mediaeval texts (cf. Langlois, *op. cit.*, p. 127), though with particular reference to the far regions of India. This custom is attributed to different peoples, all, however, placed at the ends of the earth (cf. Marco Polo, *The Book*, etc., Vol. II, p. 486, n. 3; Yule-Cordier, *Cathay*, Vol. III, p. 259, n. 2). The only traveller who recalled this custom was Friar John of Marignolle (cf. *Sinica franciscana*, etc., published by P. Anastasius van den Wyngaert, Quaraechi-Firenze, 1929, Vol. I, p. 548), but it is probable that, being inclined /towards fables and the wonders of literary and learned traditions, he drew his information from the usual sources. The great Asiatic markets were provided with interpreters, so that such legends are not to be referred to the actual experience of mediaeval travellers (cf. A. Hermann, *op. cit.*, p. 33).

[10] When Brunetto Latini's *Trésor* appeared, the most important reports of the missionaries had already been composed, but not yet published. For the sources of Latini's geographical lore, cf. S. Sundby, *Brunetto Latinos Levnet og Skrifter*, Kjøbenhavn, 1869 (Ital. edition, Firenze, 1884) and Paget Toynbee, " Brunetto Latini's Obligations to Solinus " in *Romania*, XXIII, 1894, p. 62 *et seq.*

[11] Yule-Cordier, *Cathay*, etc., I, p. 185 and 197 *et seq.*

In spite of the extensive silk production in the Middle East, in Italy and France, the ancient fables continued to be divulged through didactic treatises of this kind. Similarly, in the time of Marco Polo, the sea-ports and warehouses of Egypt, Syria, the Black and the Caspian Seas were peopled with Italian merchants, many of whom, like the Polo family, had established themselves permanently.[12] But it seems that the extensive commercial activity of these traders was not equalled by a corresponding alertness and fruitful curiosity as to the nature of the countries and peoples who provided them with merchandise.

Certainly not one of them felt the need of relating to his contemporaries what he knew. We may even suppose that in their lively competition, not infrequently conducted by force of arms, the Eastern merchants of all creeds and races were more prone to tell idle stories about the queer peoples whom they had seen than to describe their lands with their customs and produce. It was easy to surround with legends of the marvelous and mysterious the far-fetched origin of the strange goods in which they traded. Such were the pearls, spices

---

[12] The principal, and normal, outlet for merchandise coming from the interior of Asia was, besides the ports of Asia Minor, the metropolis of Constantinople. This city became the economic and commercial capital of the Levant after the Council of the Lateran, 1179, prohibited exchange of merchandise between Christians and Moslems. Notwithstanding this, Alexandria had remained an important center, especially in the thirteenth century and during the French invasion of what was left of the Byzantine Empire. The products of India, Ceylon and Eastern Asia arrived there by sea. In the thirteenth century, Alexandria was the chief oriental emporium of Venice. The most reliable source of our knowledge of foreign travel in the fourteenth century is to be found in Francesco Balducci Pegolotti, *La Pratica della Mercatura*, ed. by Allan Evans, Cambridge, Mass., 1937 (with useful introduction). For the Italian warehouses in the Levant, on the shores of the Black and Caspian Seas, cf. Von Heyd, *op. cit.*, and Adolf Schaube, *Handelsgeschichte der Romanischen Völker*, München-Berlin, 1906.

and precious stones which were prized, not only for their rarity and price, but also for the secret virtues they were supposed to possess, that is, their therapeutic and magic qualities.[13]

Thus we may believe that the mediaeval traders contributed rather to the tenacious persistence than to the suppression of these fabulous reports. Before Marco Polo, no one ever knew exactly whence these treasures came or how they were obtained.[14] Notwithstanding the data furnished by him, and, nearly forty years later, by the Florentine trade agent Balducci Pegolotti, about the products of distant Asiatic countries, old illusions maintaining the secret of their origin continued to be evoked for a long time.[15] This tendency was corroborated by a literary tradition which preserved unaltered the ideas and notions handed down by the ancients with regard, not only to the unexplored lands of Asia, but also to those regions more accessible to geographical and commercial experience. Merchants and mariners, for the most part illiterate men, shared these notions as they were related in popular treatises on science and history, intended, like the *Trésor* of Brunetto Latini, for the instruction of the people, and for reading aloud in churches and public squares.

These texts represent the stationary period of mediaeval general culture, in which late Hellenistic literary

[13] This is an important, and permanent, argument of the popular treatises on science (cf. Langlois, *op. cit.*, *passim*). On the charm and virtue of these stones cf. Marco Polo, *The Book*, etc., II, p. 259 and 263.

[14] Marco Polo indicated the places of origin of most of the precious wares and objects imported into Europe from Asia (cf. the index to Marco Polo, *The Book*, etc.). The systematic and comprehensive lists of all these items have been given by Francesco Balducci Pegolotti in *La Pratica della Mercatura* (cf. *supra*, n. 12) on the basis of the personal experience of this commercial agent.

[15] Pegolotti, *op. cit.*, pp. 302-305 (pearls and precious stones), p. 26 and *passim* for spices and gold.

doctrines, inherited from classical antiquity, propagated and fixed in the minds of men their notions of the Far East and of the regions bordering on it. It was mainly through poetry and only accidentally through the authority of erudite tradition, that the general public of that age, as well as the merchants and sailors, became acquainted with the natural and human aspects of Asia. Such people knew nothing of the original geographical and ethnological conceptions of Ptolemy, Strabo, Pliny, Pomponius Mela, Isidor of Seville and other leading authors in these fields. No authentic or reliable information about China, India and the Turkish peoples of Central Asia filtered through to the Western world from the most meager, confused and indirect accounts of Arab geographers and of Jewish travellers.[16] Thus, lasting fantasies of poetical imagination and old legends of obscure origin sought to satisfy the intense curiosity of

[16] The extracts from these works, regarding Central and Eastern Asia, are collected by Yule-Cordier, *Cathay*, etc., I, p. 241 *et seq.* and commented upon *ibid.*, p. 129 *et seq.* There is no trace of an influence of Arab geographers in the reports of mediaeval European travellers nor were Jewish itineraries before the sixteenth century, as e. g. that of Benjamin of Tudela, even indirectly known outside of their own religious and cultural spheres (Cf. Elkan Adler, *Jewish Travellers*, London). On the contrary, the Arabic influence is evident in the widely diffused doctrinal treatises of scholarly origin and containing the usual more or less fantastic and popular views about Asia (cf. Langlois, *op. cit.*, p. 71 *et seq.* and *passim*). The only mention of Eastern Asia in a treatise of popular character, drawn probably indirectly from Arabic geographical sources is to be found in the *Composizione del Mondo* of Ristoro d'Arezzo (last edition, Milano, Biblioteca Rara, 1864) written in 1282 and highly appreciated by contemporaries. Quoting the astronomical treatise of Alfraganus, Ristoro teaches that "the first climate begins in the East in the regions of Syn, and passes through the regions of Syn to the South where lies the city of the King of Syn, to Affir, which is the nobility of the Syn, and then proceeds to the southern regions of India" (*ed. cit.*, p. 172). It is difficult to establish if this passage concerns China (Syn). In this case this name would appear here for the first time in Western mediaeval literature wherein China is known only as Kathay. This passage has not been taken into consideration by Yule.

mediaeval society about the distant countries from which it expected both the most coveted goods and the most destructive invasions. To the Occidentals of the Middle Ages the kingdom of darkness, of fables and of marvels lay beyond the last storehouses of Italian and Greek merchants, and hence to the North in the hinterlands of the Sea of Azov, to the East in Transcaucasia, and in Armenia—that last, heroic and unhappy bulwark of oriental Christianity.

Whatever was known of the Moslem and pagan territories lying beyond the limits of Western geographical experiences was drawn almost exclusively from the fabulous deeds of Alexander the Great, as related in the popular poems of the twelfth century and in the new versions of these that appeared in the thirteenth century and even later.[17] The vogue for such romances was enormous and wide-spread, to such an extent that the popularity of the great Macedonian surpassed that of any other hero or sovereign of antiquity.[18] It was sufficient that the boy Marco Polo raise his eyes to the figure of Alexander the Great, on the north façade of St. Mark's, and see there the hero carried up to heaven

[17] For the geographical aspects of this subject a bibliography is given by J. K. Wright; for the literary history, cf. K. Voretsch, *Introduction to the Study of Old French Literature*, Halle, 1931, p. 241 and T. Storost, *Studien zur Alexandersage in der alten italienischen Literatur*, Halle, 1935. For more recent publications relating to the legend of Alexander, cf. the corresponding articles in the *Kulturwissenschaftliche Bibliographie zum Nachleben der Antike*, Warburg Institute, Leipzig and London, 1934, etc., and the texts and studies published in the *Elliot Monographs* edited by Prof. Armstrong, Princeton University.

[18] For the legend of Alexander the Great in the Oriental literatures, cf. Emilio S. Gómez, *Un texto Arabe occidental de la leyenda de Alejandro*, Madrid, 1929; Oskar v. Lemm, *Der Alexanderroman bei den Kopten*, St. Petersburg, 1903; Sir Ernest A. Wallis Budge, *The Alexander Book in Ethiopia*, London, 1933 and P. Y. Leeuven, *Maleische Alexanderroman*, Utrecht, 1937.

by griffins, to recall to his mind the well-known stories
of the " Merveilles du Désert," the Fountain of Youth,
the prophesies of the Sun-and-Moon trees placed at the
limits of the earth; of the marvelous palaces of Persia
and India; of Brahmans and Gymnosophists; of the
fabulous, strange and monstrous peoples inhabiting the
borders of the world; of magic forests and the fantastic
beasts which peopled them.[19] His memory would recall
all the fascinating legends which Greek biographers of
the first centuries of our era had grouped around the
figure of Alexander the Great, the conqueror who was
the pupil of Aristotle and the victim of his own
" desmesure."

Associated with the pagan traditions of the marvels
of the East was the Biblical imagery of the fabulous
lands of gold, incense and myrrh. These were to be
found near the terrestrial Paradise whence flowed
rivers, such as the Oxus and the Ganges, and which
marked the furthermost eastern limits of geographical
knowledge.[20] The name of the Biblical river Geon is
referred to in Marco Polo's book as the Oxus of the feats
of Alexander.[21] Similarly, the recollection of his adven-

---

[19] These are the principal episodes in the poetical history of the Macedonian as narrated in the different versions of the Greek romance
attributed to Pseudo-Callisthenes, in their mediaeval Latin translations.
in the French poem of Lambert di Tors and Alexandre de Bernay and in
the Italian, Spanish and Oriental elaborations of the legend and texts.
Some of these episodes are illustrated by A. R. Anderson, *Alexander's
Gate*, etc. (cf. n. 3 *supra*). On the iconography of "Alexander the Great's
Celestial Journey" cf. R. S. Loomis in the *Burlington Magazine*, 1918.

[20] Cf. A. Graf, " *Il mito del Paradiso Terrestro*," in *Miti, Leggende e
Superstizioni del Medio Evo*, Torino, 1892, a still unsurpassed essay on
this subject.

[21] Marco Polo, *The Book*, etc., II, p. 458 and especially p. 466. The
same river is mentioned in connection with the Euphrates and the Tigris,
as emptying into the Caspian Sea, in some of the best versions of Marco
Polo's text (Cf. Marco Polo, *Il Milione*, etc. a cura di L. Foscolo Benedetto, Firenze, 1928, p. 17 n.). All the principal rivers of Asia known in

tures serves to identify the topography of those parts
of Central Asia visited and described by the Venetian
traveller. When he reached the northern frontiers of
Persia and was among the Badakshan mountains, the
Moslems of these localities repeated to him the self-
same tales of the exploits of the Macedonian which,
together with the imaginary enchantments of Asia, had
inspired the bards of France and Italy.[22] In fact, in
journeying from Venice to the extreme limits of Bac-
triana, Marco Polo found himself still within the limits
of the ancient world. Within its boundaries the figure
of the Macedonian was, for the Christians of the West
and for the Moslems of Asia alike, the outstanding
representative and the only universal exponent of
ancient expansion and civilisation.

It is unnecessary here to study exhaustively the
reason why the figure of Alexander the Great remained
throughout vast territories inhabited by heterogeneous
peoples the common symbol of human greatness for so
long a time and through so many historical vicissitudes.
We can only suppose that this singular good fortune
depended upon the fact that this imaginary biography,
written in Greek by the Pseudo-Callisthenes, between
the second and the third centuries of our era, was translated not only into Latin whence it found its way into
the popular romances, but also into Armenian, Persian,
Syriac and Ethiopic, becoming thus the common pos-
session of all mankind. The person of the Macedonian
who was the central historical figure in narratives of
varied adventures; the partly real and partly fanciful
topographical background of his deeds; the numerous

the Middle Ages were more or less connected with the rivers of Paradise
(cf. J. K. Wright, *passim*).

[22] Cf. Yule's comment on this passage in Marco Polo, *The Book*, etc.,
I, p. 160.

fables set forth in the romance; the tendency to stress his moral character, the quantity of notions which owed their inspiration to him—these were all contributing factors to the universal and lasting diffusion of his name. Furthermore, we should take into consideration the fact that the earlier Greek romance of the Pseudo-Callisthenes abounds in Oriental motifs, which, in a new literary form, were thus restored to the peoples among whom they had originated.

Nevertheless, all this would not be sufficient to explain the vitality which the Alexandrian traditon, literary in origin and character, had in both the Christian and the Islamic worlds. The continuity and persistence of this partly historical and partly fabulous tradition does not depend upon intrinsic circumstances alone, but upon its transfusion into new civilisations which were heirs of the old. Two facts have sealed and confirmed his extraordinary and age-long glory: the first is the enthusiastic mention of Alexander made at the beginning of the first book of Maccabees, as the sovereign who " went through to the ends of the earth, and took spoils of a multitude of nations," thus initiating his Christian myth in that biblical book which most resembles the mediaeval " chansons de geste." [23] Furthermore, the Koran has exalted his glory equally in a sort of transfiguration which remained connected with the wonders and mysteries of the East.[24]

[23] The influence of this canonical biblical text on the French epic poems has been recognized by J. Bédier (*Les Légendes Épiques*). Concerning Alexander's glorification in the book of the Maccabees (I, Book I, Introduction, 1-10) and his lasting popularity in the Christian world, it should be remembered that the feast of the Seven Holy Maccabees is one of the oldest celebrated in the Roman Catholic Church, there being evidence of the cult of these Old Testament heroes already in the fourth century (Cf. A Ferria, S. J., " Della festa dei SS. Maccabei " etc. in *Civiltà Cattolica*, 1938, Ann. LXXXIX, p. 234 *et seq.*)

[24] The *Koran*, Sūra XVIII, 82 *et seq.* Here the Macedonian is associ-

The persistent and universal vitality of this historical figure, twice praised in sacred writings, served to perpetuate a mass of geographical fables which baffles every attempt at rational correction as the result of practical experience. It was impossible to dissociate even the empirical image of Asia, derived from travels and exploration, from the legendary figure of Alexander, sketched by poetic imagination.[25] This, then, is the reason why, despite commercial intercourse, diplomatic relations and direct contacts between the West and the East in peace and in war, everything relating to that continent appeared and persisted in the form of fables, as of a Utopia surrounded by poetic mystery.

The literary image of Asia was so deeply rooted in the mediaeval culture that it determined the character and the structure of Marco Polo's book. Although he had in mind composing a description of Asia on an empirical basis, it is incorrect to interpret this attempt as a result of Marco's scientific intentions.[26] He dictated the *Milione* not so much for the information of travellers, traders and cosmographers, as mainly for the enjoyment of his contemporaries who eagerly yearned for this kind of pleasant instruction in an epoch of prevailing didactic

---

ated with the legend of Gog and Magog and the peoples enclosed behind the great iron gate which he erected and which is mentioned by all Christian and Mohammedan travellers. Cf. A. R. Anderson, *Alexander's Gate*, etc., Cambridge, Mass., 1932.

[25] The principal allusions to the actual and poetic history of the Macedonian contained in Marco Polo's book relate to the Iron Gate, the site of the battle with Darius, his marriage with Roxana, the horse Bucephalus and its strain, the chains fixed by him on Adam's Peak in Ceylon, the "Arbre Sec," the Mohammedan image of Zulcarnain (i. e. Alexander the horned). Cf. for all these passages the comment of Yule in Marco Polo, *The Book*, etc., and the Introduction, p. 113 *et seq.* The influence of the romances of Alexander on Marco Polo's description of India has not yet been extensively studied.

[26] Cf. L. Foscolo Benedetto, *Marco Polo*, Firenze, 1932 (Introduction).

interests in culture and literature.[27] In fact, the first part of the book contains a sequel of entertaining and edifying stories dealing with the wonders of Bagdad, the legend of the Magi, the Old Man of the Mountain and his artificial Paradise, the *Arbre Sec* and sundry anecdotal details more or less connected with the authentic and the poetic history of Alexander the Great.[28] Thus, later on, the story of the Nestorian Unc Khan is fused with the legend of Prester John and narrated rather as a fairy-tale than as an historical event.[29] The Tartar expedition against Japan is described in the characteristic style of contemporary romances of chivalry, while the entire description of insular and continental India bears the marks of the traditional accounts which transformed those regions into a land of wonders, marvels and teratology.[30]

Thus all the positive and practical information offered

[27] This fact is attested by three independent but reliable versions of the book which contain the information that " when he (i. e. Messer Marco) was staying in the dungeon of Jene (i e. Genoa) because of the war . . . he thought he ought to compile the said book for the enjoyment of readers." Cf. Marco Polo, *The Description of the World*, publ. by A. C. Moule and P. Pelliott, London, 1938, Vol. I, p. 73. This is certainly the principal explanation of the small influence of his book on geographical and cosmographical authors of the later Middle Ages. Cf. Marco Polo, *The Book*, etc., I, Introduction, p. 129 *sq.*

[28] The direct influence of the legendary and poetic literature, connected with the traditional books about Asia, is especially strong in the description of the Western regions of the continent, more or less superficially described in the antique and mediaeval works on geography and cosmography. Beyond the limits of the ancient world Marco Polo recognized in the " Province of Tenduc " the country of Gog and Magog after having given an etymological explanation of these terms as follows: *Ung* was the name of the people of the country, and *Mungul* a name sometimes applied to the Tartars." Cf. Yule's remarks in Marco Polo, *The Book*, etc., I, p. 285 and 292 *et seq.*

[29] *Ibid.*, espec. Chapter XLVI *et seq.*

[30] In accordance with this quantity of tales of wonder all the versions of Marco Polo's book introduce this section, the third, of his description of the world with a hint at the " marvels " related in it.

by this book on the basis of personal experience and observation appears in a tidy and elaborated frame of tales of wonders of Hellenistic, biblical and Islamic origin. This circumstance determined the prevailing literary character of the book even independently of the collaboration of Rustician, a professional writer.[31] From this point of view, the title sometimes given to the book in mediaeval manuscripts and old editions as a " livres des merveilles du monde " appears quite justified and in accordance with the intention of the author and the interpretation of the public.[32]

In spite of its exceptional character and of the rich and varied details of an objective and reliable kind which it contains, Marco Polo's book is still connected in its essential scheme with the old tradition of Asiatic imagery created and propagated by the poetic history of Alexander the Great. Mandeville's forgery represents a further step and the literary conclusion of this development of a fantastic geography, supported, rather than destroyed, by the results of new discoveries and explorations. The same interrelations between authentic reports and literary motifs which contributed to the success of these standard geographical works of the Middle Ages determined the cosmographical conceptions of Columbus and his interpretation of reality in the New World.[33]

[31] Cf. on Rustician (called also Rusticien, Rusticians or Rustichello) of Pisa, Marco Polo, *The Book* etc., I, Introduction, p. *55 et seq.* This fellow-prisoner of Marco Polo at Genoa was certainly more of a simple " scribe who wrote down the travels," as Yule (*loc. cit.*) designated him.

[32] Cf. the fascimiles published by L. Foscolo Benedetto in his edition of Marco Polo, *Il Milione* and the Introduction to all versions and editions of the book.

[33] Cf. the author's essays on " What Columbus saw on Landing in the West Indies " in the *Proceedings of the Amer. Philos. Soc.*, July, 1941, and on " Ponce de Leon's Fountain of Youth " in the *Hispanic Amer. Hist. Review*, August, 1941.

II. THE RELIGIOUS AND POLITICAL
BACKGROUND

The first attempt toward a direct contact between the Western world and the Far East of which we know was owing rather to inspirations drawn from literature and from imagination than to the search for more extended commercial relations. This attempt failed, just as the first attempt to reach India by sea ended in a shipwreck,[1] but it influenced to some extent subsequent and more fortunate expeditions.

In the early days of October, 1177, almost a century before Marco Polo, there departed from Venice, never to return, the physician Philip, of the household of Pope Alexander III. His journey was directed toward undefined regions at the uttermost end of the earth: he bore with him a papal letter to Prester John, the fabulous sovereign of those faraway lands. The Pope had entrusted to him his belated reply to the famous *Letter* which was believed to have been sent in 1165 to the sovereigns of Europe by the supposed Lord of Eastern Asia.[2] In reality this letter was one of the most extraordinary mystifications known to the annals of political and literary history. Just who was the author of the supposedly authentic letter is not revealed, but its pro-

---

[1] This first nautical attempt to reach India " per mare Oceanum " is attributed to the Vivaldi brothers, Genoese mariners, who set sail in 1291 and reached the East African Coast. A critical bibliography of this enterprise has been published in the *Archivio Storico Italiano*, Vol. XCVI, 1938, p. 242.

[2] All the documents concerning the legend of Prester John are collected by Fr. Zarncke, " Der Priester Johannes " in *Abhandlungen der philosophisch-historischen Klasse der Kgl. Sächsischen Gesellschaft der Wissenschaften*, Leipzig, 1879, Vol. VI. The Letter of Alexander III is reproduced *ibid.*, p. 941 *et seq.*

found and enduring effect throughout mediaeval society and in the history of geography and explorations is well known.[3] We have to reconsider its essential tenor in order to see some aspects of the famous legend in new light.

In his letter, purporting to be authentic, the supposed sovereign of the three Indies, who professes himself a devout Christian and claims that his kingdom extends eastwards " ad solis ortum " and westward to the Tower of Babel, enumerates, in an arrogant and challenging tone, the riches and the marvels of his immense possessions. To the harassed Europe of the time of Frederick Barbarossa he offers a Utopian picture of the honest lives and the secure and peaceful affluence of his innumerable peoples all united under a theocratic government which assures them justice, peace and material and moral well-being.

Leaving aside the political implications of Prester John's letter, and limiting ourselves to its descriptive contents, we notice that all the marvels of Asia therein related revert to Hellenistic literary and doctrinal tradi-

---

[3] The most recent contributions and discussions concerning the legend of Prester John and its ramifications in literature, geography and poetry are mentioned by J. K. Wright (*op. cit.*) and Ch. V. Langlois (*op. cit.*); furthermore in the essay of Sir E. Denison Ross in *Travel and Travellers of the Middle Ages*, edit. by A. P. Newton, New York, 1930; finally in the writings of the author which are devoted to this subject matter, i. e. " Der Brief des Presbyters Johannes " in *Historische Zeitschrift*, Vol. CXIV, 1931, pp. 1-18; *Storia letteraria delle Scoperte Geografiche*, Firenze, 1937, p. 194 *et seq.* and " I Cantari dell'India di Giuliano Dati " in *La Bibliofilia*, Vol. XL, 1938, fasc. 8/9. The cartographic aspects of the legend are considered in the work especially devoted to the evolution of geography, e. g. Sir R. Beazley, *The Dawn of Modern Geography*, 3 vols., London, 1897-1906, espec. Vol. II; George H. T. Kimble, *Geography in the Middle Ages*, London, 1938. Lynn Thorndike has completed the list of manuscripts of the *Letter of Prester John*, published by Zarncke, *op. cit.*, in the 2nd vol. of the *History of Magic and Experimental Science*, New York, 1923, Ch. XLVII.

tions which accord with the many fanciful geographical and ethnological tales to be found in the cycle of Alexander's legendary biography. And thus, according to this widely circulated letter, Eastern Asia appears to be populated by peoples of every faith except Moslems, and also by Satyrs, Fauns, Pygmies, Cynocephali, Giants, Monoculi and Cyclopes; by Amazons and Brahmans and other strange peoples who live in territories bordering on the Terrestrial Paradise, or on the shores of rivers where gold and endless quantities of precious and magic stones are to be found, or in magnificient, enchanted forests filled with wild beasts, or in the vast expanses of fabulous countries abounding in milk and honey, where miraculous herbs grow, and also the most valued spices, and all plants useful to man. Such was the usual conception of Eastern Asia which prevailed in European literature and scholarship until the first actual explorations—and even long after them.

A few elements of this fantastic geographical image seem to stand in a certain relationship to the reality of life and civilisation within Asia. The religious tolerance of Prester John is a characteristic trait of the rulers and peoples of Central Asia and the Far East. The hostility towards the Saracens corresponds to the policy and the campaigns of the Central-Asiatic Turkish tribes in the middle of the twelfth century. Likewise the existence of some Christian peoples and rulers at the borders of the Far East is unquestionable. As a matter of fact, the most precious goods traded in Western European markets were of Asiatic origin. The entire fanciful picture of Asia displayed in the famous *Letter* has its realitistic support in all these facts and events vaguely known in the Near East and, through indirect information, even in Rome.

All this would have had a secondary, anecdotal value,

had it not been for the letter of Pope Alexander III which seemed to confirm and sanction these fantasies. According to contemporary sources, the message of the Pope was one of the circular letters sent by him " per universas gentium nationes " to announce the council which was to take place in 1178.[4] It is a curious fact, never yet noticed, that this exchange of letters in a purely imaginary world, though it was thought at the time to be real, has precisely the same tone of those messages which actually were exchanged in the course of the thirteenth century between the Mongolian Khans and the Roman Pontiffs.[5] These authentic letters of the Genghiskhanides were worded in the same insolent and provocative style which is characteristic of the apocryphal letter of Prester John addressed to the Greek Emperor, the Pope and Frederick Barbarossa. On the other hand, Alexander III, seeking to draw the legendary ruler of Asia into the fold of the Church, used the same calm and dignified tone characteristic of all messages sent by his successors to the pagan rulers of Asia.[6]

The great Pontiff of the Lombard League, having emerged victorious from the struggle against Barbarossa, attempted, in his reply to Prester John, to extend his spiritual dominion to the farthest ends of the earth, warning the fabulous sovereign to be " less inflated with pride in his opulence and power," to acknowledge the principles of the true faith, and to receive his legate in the person of his beloved son, " Magister

---

[4] Cf. Fr. Zarncke, *op. cit.*, p. 940.

[5] These letters are published by P. Pelliot, *Mongols et Papes au XIII*^e *et XIV*^e *siècles*, Paris, 1922 and " Les Mongols et la Papauté," *Revue de l'Orient Chrétien*, 1922 *et seq.*

[6] For these letters and for the policy of the Roman Pontiffs towards the Mongols, cf. besides the already quoted works, the extensive account of Giovanni Sorrento, *Il Papato, l'Europa Cristiana e i Tartari*, Milano, 1930, with ample bibliography.

Philippus," his physician, and a member of his household.

Who this first precursor of Marco Polo was we know only from references to him in the Pope's letter which was written from the Papal chancery at Venice " in rivo alto." [7] In any case Philip must have been a notable personage. Alexander III. describes him, in this short letter, as a cautious, clever, circumspect and prudent man, " in sacred doctrine most fully versed," and intrepid to the point of daring, as the Pope says, " all the strain and the different dangers of things and countries among barbarous and unknown tongues." [8] We can deduce from his official titles that he was a learned man and a diplomat rather than a church-dignitary or a missionary. Hence it follows that the Pope expected from him some reliable information about the Prester, based on the personal observation of an experienced and well-prepared man.

We gather, besides, that Master Philip must have been in the East previously, as he had kept the Pope informed of certain conversations on faith and Christian doctrine which had taken place between himself and some honored personages, supposed to be subjects of Prester John. Master Philip had probably come in contact with Nestorian and Jacobit ecclesiastics somewhere in Palestine or in the neighboring countries then under Christian rule.[9] These Asiatic Christians formed

[7] An attempt to identify this envoy was made by Ch. V. Langlois, *op. cit.*, p. 74, who supposes that he might have been the same Master Philip who translated into Latin that widely diffused Oriental treatise on medicine and hygiene known by the name of *Secretum Secretorum*. But this supposition is only upheld by the identity of name and title, both denominations being very common. Cf. about this author, L. Thorndike, *A History of Magic*, etc., Vol. II, p. 244 *et seq.* and p. 270.

[8] Fr. Zarncke, *op. cit.*, p. 943.

[9] For the contacts of the Nestorians of Central and Eastern Asia

an extensive *diaspora* scattered throughout the whole continent as far as Korea and Southern India, where they centered around the traditional tomb of Saint Thomas the Apostle.[10] The story of Prester John, of his riches, his peoples and armies, had long been familiar in the Holy Land, and, since it centered round the tomb of the Apostle of India, it is probable that it was originally a Nestorian legend, or at least a fable used by Asiatic Christians to signify the political and spiritual dominion which they temporarily exercised in Central Asia, India and the Far East.

It has been supposed that the papal legate turned his steps towards Ethiopia, which was considered in mediaeval geography as part of India and to be entirely inaccessible at that time.[11] Thus several scholars have attempted to prove that the legend of Prester John refers rather to the Negus than to any real or imaginary sovereign of India Central Asia or the Far East.[12] But until the middle of the fourteenth century all texts and maps agree in assigning him to Asia, and no one of these sources indicated that Prester John was a black king ruling over a Negro people.[13] No mediaeval author

with the western regions of the Continent, cf. F. Nau, *L'expansion nestorienne en Asie*, Paris, 1914; A. C. Moule, *Christians in China*, etc., London, 1930 and the article "Nestoriens" in the *Dictionnaire de Théologie Catholique* of Vacant and Mangenot.

[10] The legend of Prester John is strictly connected with the memory of the Sanctuary of Thomas the Apostle in India (cf. Fr. Zarncke, *op. cit.*, p. 813 *et seq.*, p. 917 and *passim*). For the legend which ascribes the origin of Christianity in the Far East to St. Thomas cf. A. C. Moule, *Christians in China*, etc., p. 10 *et seq.* Marco Polo's report about the shrine of the apostle in India, is commented upon by Yule in *The Book*, etc., II, p. 321 *et seq.*, pp. 341, 353 *et seq.* and *passim*.

[11] Cf. Fr. Zarncke, *op. cit.*, p. 945 *et seq.*; Denison Ross *Prester John*, *loc. cit.*, p. 130 *et seq.*

[12] Denison Ross, *op. cit.*, p. 184; C. Marinescu in *Bulletin de l'Acad. Roumaine*, Vol. X, 1923, p. 77 *et seq.*

[13] The Franciscan missionary Johannes of Pian del Carpine, who seems

3

or document would have overlooked this detail. It may be that, at the time of the crusades, some representatives of the Coptic church were in Jerusalem, and that some knowledge of a Christian people of " India " might have been drawn from that source. But all the travellers of the thirteenth century and Marco Polo himself located the legendary sovereign in the interior of Asia. We may presume therefore that Philip went from Venice to the Holy Land, to obtain there, from the Christians of different sects, more exact information, before setting forth into the unknown lands of Asia whence he never returned.

*   *   *

This episode closes what we may call the " mythical " period of the precursors of Marco Polo. But although succeeding periods imposed a more realistic view of Asia, yet some traces of the literary and legendary conceptions still clung tenaciously; so much so, that not until the end of the fourteenth century did the figure of Prester John of Asia disappear from Western imagination. Even to Marco Polo, Prester John was an historical and his kingdom a geographical reality, an object of lively curiosity and one of the most attractive personalities of the Eastern world. As the Christians of Asia knew but little about this legendary figure, it is certain that the Venetian traveller, as well as his precursors, set out for Asia with the image of these wonderful lands sketched by European tales and accepted throughout the Western world.[14]

to identify Prester John with Sultan Talaluddin of Khwarezm, a region between the Caspian Sea and the Amur-Daria River in Asia, calls Ethiopia " India minor," adding that the Ethiopians " nigri sunt Sarraceni." Cf. *Sinica francisc.*, p. cx *et seq.* and p. 59.

[14] For the opinions of the missionaries of the fourteenth century about Prester John, cf. *Sinica francisc.*, p. cix *et seq.*; for Marco Polo, cf. the comment of Yule in *The Book*, etc. I, p. 231 *et seq.* and *passim.*

Nevertheless, events of immense importance had occurred to transform this edifying and poetic myth into a concrete and terrifying reality. In the interval of nearly seventy years between the failure of this first embassy to a fabulous monarch and the more successful papal missions to a real sovereign of Asia, the political structure of the Asiatic continent had changed completely with a loss of much of the ancient traditions of its civilisations, its faith and its prestige. During this interval Genghis Khan had unified the peoples and territories reaching from the Yellow Sea to the Black Sea, sowing death and destruction, and creating the most extensive empire recorded in history. After him his sons and grandsons temporarily pushed the boundaries of his dominions as far as the Adriatic (1241), creating a system of Mongolian states depending, either actually or nominally, upon the Grand Khan, Genghis's successor. Thus were gathered together under a single régime of violence and menace the nomadic and the fixed populations, the barbarous and the civilized, the ancient and the new, of an entire continent, so that the Grand Khan's possessions and influence extended from Asia Minor to Korea, and from Siberia to the Persian Gulf, the Himalayas and Malaysia. At that time a safe-conduct granted by the one and only authority in the form of the famous " golden tablet " enabled the traveller to journey from the Mediterranean or from the Baltic to the Eastern limits of the world, connected with the West by a continuous system of post routes, perfectly efficient in times of war and peace.[15]

Thus, contrary to what had been foreseen, the fair

[15] A reproduction and description of these " golden tablets " is given by Yule in his commentary to Marco Polo, *The Book*, etc., I, p. 351 *et seq.* A detailed map of Asia under the Mongols in A. Hermann, *A historical and commercial Atlas of China*, Cambridge, Mass., 1935 (N. 54).

Utopian and literary dreams of the universal empire of Prester John had rapidly become a grim historic and political reality. Genghis Khan and his successors aspired to the dominion of the world, and they neglected no occasion to proclaim to the rest of humanity the mission which they believed themselves destined to fulfill. These barbarous and bloody conquerors, who had reduced flourishing cities to heaps of ashes, burying beneath them innumerable innocent victims, works of art and historic dynasties, had, nevertheless, the virtue of religious tolerance. This characteristic attitude toward religion in general and, on the other hand, the different creeds of their empire, is a capital problem in the understanding of these newly-attempted intercontinental relations. The travels of Marco Polo did not start as a commercial enterprise but as a mission intended to propagate the Christian faith in the Far East.

The tolerance of the Khans had a spiritual as well as a political inspiration. They knew better than the Western rulers that imperial expansion and religious intolerance are contradictory terms which exclude each other. Consequently the Khans anxiously prevented in their territories every disturbance of the religious peace that might have been caused by public controversies, noisy competition, zealous proselytism, discrimination and persecution. In this empire Christians of the Nestorian, Jacobit and Greek churches, Moslems, Manichaeans, Jews, Buddhists, Lamaists, Taoists, idolaters of different kinds and later some Roman Catholic missionaries were allowed to practice their rites and to teach their doctrines, but religious discussions were rare and isolated events. When the Grand Khan allowed the Franciscan missionary William of Rubruk to argue with the priests of other creeds before a great concourse of people on Pentecost eve 1253 at the capital of the Mongolian empire, the Buddhists "began to murmur against Mangu Khan, the emperor, for no other Khan attempted to pry into their secrets." [16]

The attitude of the Orientals toward religious controversies was quite different from that of the Europeans who eagerly sought every occasion for theological discussions with persons of a different faith.[17] The Christians of Asia shared with all other Orientals the dislike of such mostly idle and always unpleasant disputes. When Rabban Sauma the Nestorian priest, born within the limits of China, went to Rome in 1287, he was pressed by his hosts into a strictly theological discussion which he ended by saying: "I am come from distant lands not to discuss or to preach my belief, but to pay my respects to my Lord the Pope and to the relics of the Saints. . . . If you please, let us have done with discussions."[18] In the Orient many missionaries have paid with their lives for their excessive fervor for public disputes on religious matters.

For the Mongolian Khans the substantial equivalence of all the religions was a fundamental maxim of their policy. In certain circumstances, the priests and representatives of these different creeds were admitted to the presence of the sovereigns as exorcisers and soothsayers or as intercessors and mediators of divine assistance and inspiration. Apart from this clear-sighted political purpose, this benevolent religious neutrality may be explained by the fact that the Genghiskhanides were all heathen and idolaters by origin, tradition and confession. It lay in the polytheistic essence of their primi-

---

[16] Cf. *Sinica francisc.*, p. 294; Rockhill, *The Journey*, etc., p. 231.

[17] E. Kantorowitz, *Frederick the Second*, New York, 1931, p. 346 *et seq.*, gives some fine examples of these significant tournaments.

[18] A. C. Moule, *Christians in China*, etc., p. 108.

tive religion that these powerful rulers accepted without conflicts, or even hesitation, the most heterogeneous forms of alien worship, and connected indifferently the symbolism of sublime spiritualistic religions with the crudest expressions of barbarous superstitions.

This attitude was totally incomprehensible to the Western Christians who came in contact with the Mongolian world. Consequently the history of these contacts is a sequel of misunderstandings and of failures. As a matter of fact, only monotheistic religions are essentially intolerant exclusive and fanatical. Polytheism has no limits to its power of adoption. This is the deepest explanation of the Mongolian policy of toleration, acceptance and benevolence toward all creeds; a policy supported by a rudimentary but wise philosophy expressed by the Khans themselves to their bewildered Christian guests. A day after the public discussion between Friar William of Rubruk and the representatives of the different Asiatic religions, the Emperor told the missionary that " as God gives us the different fingers of the hand, so he gives to men divers ways . . . God gave you (*i. e.* the Christians) therefore the Scriptures, and you do not keep them; He gave us (*i. e.* the Mongols) diviners, we do what they tell us, and we live in peace." [19] Just a generation later Kubilai Khan explained to the Polos at Peking that " the Christians say their God is Jesus Christ, the Saracens Mahomet, the Jews Moses, the idolaters Sogomoni Borcan (*i. e.* Sakyamuny Buddha) . . . . And I do honour and reverence to all four, that is to him who is the greater in heaven and more true, to him I pray that he may help me." [20]

[19] Cf. *Sinica francisc.*, p. 298; Rockhill, *The Journey*, etc., p. 236.
[20] This passage, undoubtedly authentic, is preserved only in Ramusio's

It is only from this angle of spiritual things that it is possible to understand the development of the mostly unpleasant relations between East and West in the epoch of the Mongolian domination. Since the Genghis-khanides did not possess a civilisation of their own to propagate and defend, we see them remaining Shaman-ists in Mongolia, becoming Moslems in Persia and Buddhists in China, and surrounding themselves every-where, without any prejudices of race and faith, with the representatives of all the sects and religions which then abounded throughout Asia. But none of them, not even the Tartar sovereigns of the " Golden Horde " which bordered on the Greek and Roman Catholic world, ever became Christians, or even seriously thought of being converted. The Christians were a small and comparatively unimportant minority in this vast empire, and no one of its rulers felt the political necessity of accepting the baptism of Christ.[21]

Notwithstanding this and in spite of repeated, painful and humiliating disillusionments, it was a common be-lief, throughout all that century among the monarchs and peoples of the West, that one or another of the Mongol chiefs, perhaps even the Grand Khan himself, was a Christian. Or at least the hope was cherished that it would not be a difficult undertaking to bring them and even all their subjects into the fold of the Church. The further reasons for this age-long misunder-standing are many and complex, but they must be taken into consideration if we would understand the intent, the expectations and the achievements of the prede-

version of Marco Polo, *Description*, etc., I, p. 202; *Il Milione*. p. 70 n.; *The Book*, etc., I, p. 348 n.; A. C. Moule, *Christians in China*, p. 135.

[21] P. Pelliot, " Chrétiens d'Asie Centrale et d'Extreme Orient," in *T'oung Pao*, 1914, p. 263 *et seq*., and A. C. Moule, *op. cit.*

cessors of Marco Polo and even the conditions of his own
more fortunate enterprise.

Meanwhile it should be remembered that the Western
belief in the existence of innumerable Christian peoples,
inhabiting Far Eastern Asia, was confirmed not only by
the widely known apocryphal *Letter of Prester John*,
translated into several tongues, but also by the letter
of Alexander III which had found its way into the
chronicles of the thirteenth century. Apart from the interests of the groups of Nestorians in Syria and Palestine
to maintain this general conviction, it is known that
since 1141 the Crusaders had attributed the military
victories of the Kitans led by Ye-lu-ta-shi, over the
Moslems in Turkestan and the northern provinces of
Persia to a Christian king and his successors.[22]

When, later on, Genghis Khan had reached the apex
of his power, after forty years of warfare which had
rendered his lands inaccessible to Moslems and Christians alike, that terrible Tartar leader was considered,
in the Holy Land, and by the Crusaders in Egypt and
Europe, as the descendant and heir of Prester John and
consequently as an eventual ally in their struggle against
the Saracens.[23] Appalling as was the desolation wrought
by the Tartars within the boundaries of the Christian
world, still it was considered that the Moslems had been
even more harshly and radically dealt with by them.
This gave rise to hopes of obtaining Tartar help against
the common enemy, especially because there was now
felt to be no doubt as to the existence of innumerable
Christians living undisturbed in the Tartar dominions.

These illusions contained the shadow of an undeniable

---

[22] All the documents concerning this stage of the legend are collected
by Fr. Zarncke, *op. cit.*, II *Abhandlung*, p. 6 *et seq.*

[23] Fr. Zarncke, *op. cit.*, p. 850 *et seq.*, 863 *et seq.*; Denison Ross, *op.
cit.*, p. 182.

fact, which is that there really existed in Northern Mongolia, subject to the Grand Khan, the Keraits, a Nestorian people whose ruling dynasty was connected with the Genghis Khan family through marriages and had maintained in it some Christian influence, even throughout succeeding generations.[24] The Naimans and Uigurs were other neighboring tribes with prevailing Nestorian populations subjugated by the Mongols in their early expansion.[25] The Christian influence, however, should not be overrated, for it is certain that only the women of the Genghis Khan family professed the Nestorian faith. Moreover the priests and prelates admitted into the various Mongolian courts were more intent on obstructing than on favoring the penetration of Catholicism into Asia. This explains why the Franciscan missionaries, besides relating indisputable facts observed by them, were prone to speak severely and disparagingly of these heretics, calling them a " corrupt, ignorant, simoniacal, superstitious and lying people." [26]

But before the institution of the Catholic missions " ad Tartaros " such things could not be known. Actual contacts with that far-away world were rare and superficial, whereas the illusions were tenacious. The events of 1241 which, for a short time, put Western Europe into immediate and direct contact with the Tartars, dissipated imaginative fancies and replaced them by a more realistic and solid conception of what Asia really was. The Tartar expansion westward involved Eastern Europe in a devastating cataclysm and pressed down

[24] Cf. P. Pelliot, *Chrétiens d'Asie*, etc., p. 623 *et seq.*

[25] Another important Nestorian tribe in Mongolia was the Öngüt. A short but comprehensive survey of Mongolian ethnography and history has been published by Paul Pelliot in the *Enciclopedia Italiana*, art. " Mongoli."

[26] *Sinica francisc.*, p. 233, 238, 346 *et seq.*, and *passim*.

through Hungary to the gates of Italy. Fortunately for her the conquerors retired beyond the Dnieper, leaving to the sovereigns of Europe and to the Roman Curia the task of warding off further danger and of planning for defense. At this time began the systematic exploration and penetration of interior and Eastern Asia, of which Marco Polo was the champion.[27]

[27] For the political reaction following the Mongolian invasion of Eastern and Central Europe, cf. G. Soranzo, *Il Papato, l'Europa Cristiana e i Tartari* quoted *supra*.

III. THE MISSIONS "AD TARTAROS"[1]

The merit of the great initiative called "the missions ad Tartaros" belongs to the Genoese Sinibaldo Fieschi, who was elected Pope in June 1243 and took the name of Innocent IV. He introduced into papal policy the diplomatic methods of his own city, directing it towards the spiritual conquest of Asia.[2] Before the Council of Lyons had decreed the missions "ad Tartaros," Innocent IV had already sent an ambassador of his own choice to the Mongolian Emperor on his personal initiative in the person of the Franciscan Friar John of Pian del Càrpine, of the county of Perugia. The continuity of papal aims and methods, in spite of the novelty of the enterprise, is owing to the fact that in choosing Friar John, a man whom he completely trusted, the Pope was following exactly, and probably intentionally, the procedure of Alexander III who had named Master Philip his legate *a latere*. Salimbene in his celebrated chronicle styles him "familiaris homo et spiritualis et literatus et magnus prolocutor et in multis expertus,"

[1] All the reports of the Franciscan missionaries of Central and Eastern Asia are now collected with Introduction, explanatory notes and extensive bibliography in Vol. I of the *Sinica franciscana*. Hakluyt's translations of the oldest and principal reports are reprinted by C. R. Beazley, *The Texts and Versions of John de Plano Carpini and William Rubruquis,* London, 1903, and in the appendix of the edition of Mandeville's *Travels,* London, 1905. Important sections of other travellers are in Rockhill's edition of William of Rubruck, *op. cit.*,—for the Dominican missions, cf. B. Altaner, *Die Dominikanermissionen des 13. Jahrhunderts,* Habelschwerdt, 1924. Bibliographical notes concerning more recent publications will be found in the *International Geographical Bibliography.* An excellent condensation of the principal reports is in the second volume of Beazley's *Dawn of Modern Geography.*

[2] Cf. the corresponding sections of G. Soranzo, *Il Papato, l'Europa Cristiana e i Tartari,* Milano, 1930 with a rich bibliography of the subject.

a man, in short, particularly fitted for this unusual task and in all things similar to his first and unhappy predecessor.[3] Like him, Friar John was charged not only with investigating the affairs of the Tartars and other Oriental peoples and with informing the Curia of the power and intentions of the Khans, but also, it would seem, with inviting them to become Christians and recognize the supremacy of the Roman Pontiff. The Pope trusted in the versatility, intelligence and eloquence of his envoy.

Friar John is to all intents the first effectual precursor of Marco Polo. No one before him had ventured beyond the borders of the ancient world, nor penetrated so far into the interior of Asia. The account of his travels, entitled *Historia Mongalorum*, is written in a style hitherto unknown to mediaeval Western literature and of which the *Milione* became the masterpiece. It is an empirical description of the inhabitants and regions of Asia, and at the same time an itinerary. As the *Milione* acquaints us with Mongolian civilisation at the apogee of the Genghis Khan dynasty, so the book of Friar John presents this civilisation to us while it was still in the process of ascending and when Chinese, Persian and Byzantine influences had hardly begun to alter the native traditions of this nomad people who were destined to conquer much of the world. Furthermore this extensive report contains the earliest history of an Asiatic people unaltered by the usual padding of fables, legends and commonplaces from ancient times.

The *Historia Mongalorum* was inserted a few years after its appearance in the *Speculum* of Vincent of Beauvais, and has been so often edited, translated,

---

[3] Salimbene, *Cronica* in *Monum. Germaniae Historica*, Scriptores, Vol. XXXII, p. 206.

commented upon and illustrated, that we may limit ourselves here to considering its character and its author in their relations to the more restricted field of our present interests.[4] Friar John left Lyons on Easter Day 1245, crossed Bohemia, Poland and Russia, travelling always " from outpost to outpost " in Tartar territory. Almost a year later, he reached the horde of Batu, son of the eldest son of Genghis Khan, and Lord of the Western Tartars. This powerful prince, who was the conqueror of Hungary, had now pitched his camp on the shores of the lower Volga. Thence, accompanied always by Friar Benedict the Pole, himself the author of a short account of the same journey, Friar John proceeded, amid untold hardships, across the desolate steppes between the Caspian Sea and the Lake of Aral.[5] After having passed the destroyed cities lying along the Sirdaria and having crossed the region of Kara-Kitai and the country of the Naimans, he finally arrived in Mongolia on July 22, 1246. The Imperial court was then encamped a half-day's journey from Karakorum, the capital of the Mongolian empire.

He found, on his arrival, that a vast number of princes, dignitaries, ambassadors and folk of every tongue and faith, were awaiting the election and con-

---

[4] The *Speculum historiale* of Vincent of Beauvais (last edition, Douai, 1624) was published between 1256 and 1259, i. e. a few years after Friar John wrote his report. But the *Historia Mongalorum* was certainly diffused in many separate manuscripts, as we can infer from the account of the famous chronicler Salimbene of Parma who tells us that Friar John was wont to give his book to read whenever he was pressed to tell stories about the Tartars, and that, on the other hand, he explained and discussed details when the readers were not able to understand or when they showed their astonishment at the facts related. Cf. *Monumenta Germaniae Historica*, Scriptores, Vol. XXXII, p. 207.

[5] The text of the short report of Benedict the Pole in *Sinica francisc.*, pp. 133-143; English translation by Rockhill, *The Journey*, etc., p. 33 et seq.

secration of Küyük as Grand Khan of the Tartars, and that the regency of his mother Turakina was about to come to an end. One of the first official acts of the new Emperor was to receive the papal envoys and to prepare a minute draft of his haughty and vague reply to the Pope.[6] The original copy of it is still preserved in the Vatican archives. Taking with them this precious document, the legates set out upon their return journey after having spent four months in the imperial camp where they had been able to observe many things for themselves and to learn of many more from others. Upon his return to Lyons in November 1247, Friar John made a full report of his mission both by word of mouth and in writing to the Pope and to the Curia. As a reward for his achievements he was appointed to the Bishopric of Antivari, where he died on August 1, 1252. His name was later enrolled in the glorious Franciscan martyrology.

This pioneer of Asiatic exploration has always been the object of much and well-deserved admiration. A great traveller, heavily built, in the habit of moving about astride a Franciscan donkey, he was obliged to accustom himself to travelling, at a great speed, from one Tartar post to another, strapped on to their fast horses. At all seasons he braved the most inclement weather, the most disgusting food, the vexations and humiliations inflicted upon him by Tartar functionaries; he witnessed the savage cruelties of their lords and their armies, expecting at any moment to become their victim. But besides the physical hardihood and spiritual strength which enabled him, as well as his companion, to brave not only these dangers, but also to overcome the peril of deserts, steppes, impassable mountains,

---

[6] Cf. the text of this letter in *Sinica francisc.*, p. 141 *et seq.*

tempests and other inconveniences, we must admire the intellectual vigor with which he set aside prejudices, commonplaces and traditional illusions which were held in this time with regard to the regions and peoples of Asia.

Without doubt during the decades which preceded this memorable journey, both direct and indirect experiences had taught men to consider these matters in a more realistic spirit. But if we think, for example, of the illusions of the King of France who in those years still cherished the delusion of receiving help from the interior of Mongolian Asia—or if we recall the notions about the Asiatic continent, and even of the land bordering on Palestine, which were published in contemporary chronicles as well as in doctrinal and poetic literature—then the realism of Friar John appears as one of the most notable intellectual conquests of his century.[7] In his book a recollection of the marvels of Asia is found only in the mention of the Cynocephali, the Monopodes and other monsters who are relegated to Arctic regions and desert wastes.[8] The existence of these monsters is attested by Isidore of Seville, the only author, whom Friar John quotes, and by many authors, but he seems to follow more recent mediaeval traditions when he associated the views of monstrous races with the northern lands.[9]

[7] King Louis IX's sentiments and expectations are related by Joinville, *Vie de St. Louis*, publ. by N. de Wailly, 2d ed. Paris, 1906. For the opinions of the curiosities and marvels of the countries bordering on the Holy Land, cf. J. K. Wright, *op. cit.*, and the compilation of L. Dresbach, *Der Orient in der altfranzoesischen Kreuzzugsliteratur*, Breslau, 1901.

[8] *Sinica francisc.*, pp. 60, 74 *et seq.*, 111, 138.

[9] For this tendency and its evolution, cf. the article of Eva Matthews Sanford, " Ubi lassus deficit orbis " publ. in the *Philological Quarterly*, Vol. XIII, 1932, p. 357 *et seq.* William of Rubruck, a few years later, again localized these monstrous races in the Arctic regions of Asia (cf. *Sinica francisc.*, p. 269 and Rockhill, *The Journey*, etc., p. 198).

Friar John places the kingdom of Prester John beyond the Indus—and thus locates it very differently from Marco Polo and other Asiatic explorers—and he contributes new data toward the verification of the existence of this imaginary kingdom and toward stimulation of curiosity about it.[10] In presenting to us the Chinese as " homines benigni et humani " he agrees with the picture which Pliny and other authors had given of the " amiable and peaceable " Seres, a people who, according to ancient geographers, were most frugal, and lovers of a tranquil life, although expert in the use of arms and in warfare.[11] By saying of them that, though pagans, they possess the Old and New Testaments, the Lives of the Fathers, churches and convents in which God is adored and Christ is worshipped,[12] it is evident that Friar John adapted the information which he had received from widely prevailing ideas, held from remotest times, of the existence, in the Far East, of a people notable for their intelligence and civic virtues.

This image was so deeply rooted in the geographical conceptions of the Western world that about three centuries later Bishop Bartolomé de Las Casas, friend of Columbus and historian of his enterprise, repeatedly compared the good-natured and simple natives of the Bahamas and of the Antilles with those fabulous people dwelling at the Eastern borders of the world.[13] The

[10] *Sinica francisc.*, p. 110 *et seq.* and p. 59.

[11] It is well known that William of Rubruck was the first western writer to identify Cathay with the classical country of the Seres (Rockhill, *The Journey*, etc., p. 155 n.; *Sinica francisc.*, p. 236), but the term " terra Kytaorum " appears in Friar John's report as inhabited by an equally pious, friendly and industrious people as the Seres are described by classical authors. Cf. Yule-Cordier, *Cathay*, etc., I, p. 185 *et seq.*, 196 *et seq.*, and 203 *et seq.*

[12] *Sinica francisc.*, p. 57 *et seq.*

[13] Cf. Bartolomé de las Casas, "Apologetica historia de las Indias," in

" just Ethiopians " of Homer, the Brahmans of the legend of Alexander the Great, the Seres of the Latin authors were three different aspects of the same idea about this Far East Utopia to be found in ancient literature and geography. The legend of Prester John and of his happy empire is the Christian and mediaeval metamorphosis of this old conception which continued to exist and to influence the interpretation of reality and actual experience.[14] Obviously, a " literatus et magnus prolocutor et in multis expertus " of Friar John's kind was extensively acquainted with these traditions, and he lent his ear to this early information concerning the peoples of the East because he found therein the confirmation of firmly accepted beliefs. Disappointed by what he saw among the Mongols and the peoples of Central Asia, he simply shifted beyond their Eastern borders the actuality of the image of an ideal people who needed only baptism to become Christian in essence and form.

As for the rest, Friar John's exhaustive report is concerned with his direct observations, or with information obtained from local even if not always reliable sources. The vast store of information which he collected by experience and investigation about a world so remote from his own, is arranged in an organized and orderly fashion. The account opens with a rapid description of the continent, followed by several chapters on the

Nueva Biblioteca de Autores Españoles, Vol. XIII, Madrid, 1909, p. 448 and *passim*. The assertion of Aeneas Sylvius (*Historia Rerum Ubique Gestarum*, 1477) that the people of China are very mild and peaceable prompted Columbus to believe " that the natives of Asia would make no trouble for a conqueror." Cf. S. E. Morison, *The Admiral of the Ocean Sea. A Life of Christopher Columbus*, Boston, 1942, I, p. 124.

[14] Cf. the author's essay on " Dante e l'Oriente " in *Giornale Dantesco*, Vol. XXXIX (N. S. IX), 1938, p. 79 *et seq.*

nations, religions and customs of the Tartars. Then comes an ample account of their origin and history, concluding with a minute analysis of the military and political organization which enabled this people without historical background and legislation to establish, extend and administer such an immense empire. This enumeration of particulars culminates in a long chapter, the seventh, which possesses all the characteristics of a diplomatic report intended to give information, details and counsel on the manner of defending the European peoples from the danger which the Mongolian Empire really constituted for Western civilisation. Only at the end, as an appendix, does Friar John trace his itinerary, writing in the first person of the adventures he had encountered on his journey and his recollections of them. He describes, as an eye-witness, anecdotes and gossip of the Grand Khan's court, tells of its seat in that city of tents, which then harbored the ruler, and portrays its ceremonial, dignity and usages.

Such was the first authentic description of the Mongolian Empire. Aside from the few fables at which it hints, it contains nothing improbable, so much so that its documentary value has been long since proved. When interpreted by the methods of philological and historical criticism, this work represents one of the main sources for Asiatic history of its epoch. Realizing how different his clear and truthful account of remotest Asia must seem to his contemporaries who were accustomed to quite another conception of that continent, Friar John repeatedly assures his readers of the veracity of his statements and, at the end of his book, before calling on God as his witness, he names those persons who were competent to affirm that he had really returned from the far-away regions which he had described.

He drew his knowledge of the history of the Mongolian Empire mainly from indirect and, of course, from oral information, most of it being gathered probably from among his Tartar advisers and the Christians living at the Imperial court.[15] The scanty and sometimes confused or even erroneous geographical details contained in his book prove that the Friar had little interest in this field when it was detached from the historical and political objectives of his exploration. Even in this case his statements are mostly accidental and indirect, generally depending on information received from his native fellow travellers or on misleading geographical conceptions of learned origin and character. Thus, *e. g.*, he reveals for the first time the local names of the principal rivers of Russia, but on the other hand he did not recognize that the Caspian was an inland sea, independent of the Black Sea.[16]

Except for the climate, which he describes impressively in the introduction to his report, the Friar is not especialy attracted by the natural aspects of Asia. There is no word in the whole book which may reveal his personal reaction towards the landscapes or any particular scenery of the continent. Only parenthetically does he speak of the " beautiful plain " where the emperor's camp was erected.[17] This may be a common attitude of mediaeval travellers which corresponds to the general indifference of contemporary writers and artists toward natural aspects. But there are some striking exceptions to this common rule, and it is worth while to take them into closer consideration.

[15] *Sinica francisc.*, p. 125. One of the best informers of Friar John at the court was " a certain Ruthenian called Cosmas, a goldsmith, and a great favourite of the Emperor." *Ibid.*, p. 122 and Rockhill, *The Journey*, etc. p. 26.

[16] *Sinica francisc.*, p. 108 and 114.

[17] *Ibid.*, p. 118, 32.

Benedict the Pole, Friar John's travelling companion, seems to have had an eye for the vegetation. He related that, when crossing Comania, the country between the Don and the Volga, he "found a great deal of worm-wood (absincium)." [18] But it was a reminiscence of an Epistle of Ovid and not a particular interest in botany that directed the attention of the Friar to this rather inconsiderable plant. In fact, he explains in his report that "that country was one called Pontus, and Ovid says of Pontus

Tristia per vacuos horrent absinthia campos." [19]

This is one of the characteristic examples to be found in the history of travel literature by which we may recognize the influence of poetry and imagination on the interpretation of natural features and geographical conceptions. The only plant which the two very learned and extensively experienced men were able to observe during two and more years of travel over thousands and thousands of miles was this poor wormwood whose bitter taste had been for the unhappy Latin poet the symbol of his tormenting exile. The endless steppes of Comania reminded the Friar of those " dreary fields " and " mournful wormwoods " which Ovid had actually seen, but in a quite different country, *i. e.* on the Western shores of the Black Sea. It is not alone the geographical identification of the country which depends in this case, upon a poetic reminiscence, but even the actual interest of the traveller and his capacity to discover anything

---

[18] *Ibid.*, p. 137, 6 and Rockhill, *The Journey*, etc., p. 35.

[19] " Bitter wormwood bristles throughout the empty fields." *Epist. ex Ponto*, III, 1, 23 (a similar expression *ibid.*, VIII, 15). Friar William of Rubruck reports that wormwood was used for fuel in the tent of Mangu Khan near Karakorum asserting that it grows there to great size (cf. Rockhill, *The Journey*, etc., p. 172).

in the countless aspects of nature seen with his own eyes during his long journey.

In the history of Asiatic exploration this is not an isolated case, but a typical one. The only tree of which Marco Polo gave a detailed description after twenty-five years of travelling in Asia was the legendary "ARBRE SOL which we Christians call the *Arbre sec* " discovered by him " in the province of Tonocain in the extremity of Persia toward the North " in the country where " was fought the battle between Alexander and Darius." [20] The literary reminiscences of the Romance of Alexander and the Christian legends and poems devoted to the wood of the Holy Cross made the traveller responsive to the vegetation of this region. Never, during so many years, had this keen and restless explorer been attracted by any other tree whatsoever, although he passed through the extended oases of Central and Eastern Asia and observed the luxuriant vegetation of China and India. His interest in botany is generally limited to practical details, and then only in so far as they may concern the tradesmen of Europe. A plant in itself, however beautiful and peculiar it might have been, would not have induced him to write down a minute description of its distinguishing marks.

[20] *The Book*, etc., I, p. 127 *et seq.* with the comment of Yule. There is then another much shorter description of the Sago-tree presented by Marco Polo as a " great marvel " of the Kingdom of Fansur at Sumatra (*ibid.*, II, p. 300). In this case, the traveller was more interested in the flower of Sago some of which he brought with him to Venice (*ibid.*, p. 305). He describes the *Arbre Sec* as " a tall and thick tree, having the bark on one side green and the other white; and it produces a rough husk like that of a chestnut, but without anything in it. The wood is yellow like box, and very strong, and there are no other trees near it, nor within a hundred miles of it, except on one side, where you find trees within about ten miles' distance." In Dante's epoch a circumstantial and naturalistic description like this appears only in a spiritualistic or poetic framework.

It is only through stimulating their imaginative minds that these mediaeval travellers came to grasp the characteristic features of the countries which they visited. Without this particular sensibility, stirred up and refined by poetry and imagination, these travellers are generally blind, blunt or indifferent towards those aspects of reality which lie beyond the limits of their immediate interests and of their actual task. They share the common inclination of their contemporaries to take an interest in the objects of reality only when they can connect them with human events or with a spiritual interpretation.

Friar John's curiosity in Asiatic matters is mainly directed toward the features, habits, customs, laws, manner of living and superstitions of the exotic peoples he described, neglecting everything not closely associated with their life and history. The description he gave of the outward shape and the moral character of the Tartars has no parallel in the Latin and vulgar literature of the Middle Ages.[21] No detail of the Imperial household and court ceremonial escaped his penetrating curiosity. His sober but accurate and vivid report makes the reader participate in the colorful, swarming, tumultuous life in the huge city of tents where a teeming multitude of dignitaries, priests and warriors dwelt in the expectation of Küyük Khan's election.[22]

All this spectacular display of power and pomp did not impress the Italian Minorite very much. Friar Benedict the Pole was decidedly fascinated at the sight of the newly crowned emperor " radiant in gorgeous attire," sitting on a throne of ivory in the midst of his tent.[23] He was not insensitive to the polite and even

---

[21] *Sinica francisc.*, p. 32 *et seq.* and p. 47 *et seq.*
[22] *Ibid.*, p. 116 *et seq.* and Rockhill, *The Journey*, pp. 18-30.
[23] *Sinica francisc.*, p. 134, 10; Rockhill, *op. cit.*, p. 38.

cordial way in which the emperor's mother entertained both friars in her "great and beautiful tent." [24] But Friar John seldom uses expressions revealing a personal reaction, a naive interest or an effort toward a friendly understanding of this peculiar world. His vocabulary of words of praise does not go beyond the most conventional expressions, and even these are very scarce in his extended and detailed report.

This is not due to indifference or to a sort of scientific objectivity, but apparently it is the result of an hostile attitude which is characteristic of all the ecclesiastical precursors of Marco Polo. When we do not limit our interest in Friar John's report merely to the related facts and pay attention to the imponderable symptoms of his style and tone, then we may easily recognize the fact that he never ceased to feel himself to be the representative of a higher civilisation who viewed with contempt, and even with repulsion, the barbarous world of the Tartars. His aversion towards it begins with the country itself which he found " more miserable than he is able to describe." [25] To the few good qualities the Tartars may have had he opposes a long list of the bad habits and detestable manners of this "irascible, mendacious and malicious race of drunken liars and murderers." [26] He is horrified by their cruelty in keeping enslaved the subjugated nations and by their lack of faith and honesty as shown by their breaking promises and agreements whenever it might suit them to do so.

He speaks respectfully of the emperor as a " man very

[24] *Ibid.* Yet it must be noted that the contemporary chronicler Salimbene, who knew Friar John personally and spoke with him repeatedly after his return from Asia, related in his famous book that the Friar was received and treated by the emperor " honorifice et curialiter et benigne." *Loc. cit.*, p. 207.

[25] *Sinica francisc.*, p. 32, 6.   [26] *Ibid.*, p. 45 *et seq.*

wise, exceedingly shrewd, earnest and of grave de-
meanor, whom nobody ever saw laugh or behave himself
lightly." [27] We suspect that this exceptionally benevolent impression was inspired partially by the fact that
the friars were assured by the Christians who were of
the emperor's household " that they firmly believed that
he was about to become a Christian." [28] For the rest,
the sagacious Minorite did not watch the Tartars with
a friendly eye, and he is rather inclined to detest than
to praise them.

But every careful reader will appreciate the abundance of exact details and dispassionate information
concerning the political structure and the military or-
ganisation of the Mongolian empire. With his report
he lifted the veil of mystery that had divided the
Western world from the interior of Asia from time
immemorial. This is an extraordinary achievement in
itself. But its symptomatic value and its importance in
the history of culture and literature are increased by
the fact that this report is the first document of a
systematic and objective representation of life and
events sketched from direct experience and with a keen
sense of pertinent and essential details. Occasionally
one can find something of this kind in the best of the
contemporary chronicles. But in writing his report the
Friar could not avail himself of literary traditions and
models as the mediaeval historians always did. He
depended only on his ability and on the suggestive
power of his unadorned style.

Though he tries to give an objective and positive
description of the geographical and political features of
Asia, still he fears that he will not be believed and that

[27] *Ibid.*, p. 124; Rockhill, *op. cit.*, p. 29.
[28] *Ibid.*

he will be considered an impostor. This explains his
pathetic protests, and the list of witnesses with which
he concludes his book shows the uneasy state of mind
of a very conscientious man fully aware of his great
responsibility. So too, Marco Polo during his whole life
was unable to free himself from the suspicion of having
deceived his readers by relating so many strange and
incredible things. The famous anecdote told of Marco
Polo by the chronicler Jacopo da Acqui is illustrative
of this latent incredulity. Jacopo reports that on Marco's
death-bed his friends exhorted him to retract whatever
he had written in his book contrary to the truth, whereupon he answered that he had not recounted the half
of what he had really seen.[29] If we inquire into the
reason for such an insinuation in a society so inclined
to believe fables and so avid of the marvellous as was
the mediaeval, we may observe that credulity and
skepticism are complementary expressions, and at times
the equivalents of ignorance. In this Friar John also
proved to be a wary and cautious man, protecting himself in this way from an ill-willed and ignorant disbelief.

To his carefulness we are indebted for the preserva-
tion of the memory of several Genoese and Venetian
merchants living in Constantinople, "who came to
Russia through the Tartars," and whom he met at Kiev
on his return journey.[30] These persons were probably
fur merchants, people who, like some of the Polo family
at that time, lived in Constantinople and were fairly familiar with the Tartars who had settled or travelled
about in these far Westerly parts of their domain. Probably not one of these merchants ever penetrated beyond

[29] Cf. Yule's Introduction to Marco Polo, *The Book*, etc., p. 54. This
skeptical attitude of his contemporaries explains the small influence of
Marco Polo's book on geography and cosmography of a learned character.
[30] *Sinica francisc.*, p. 129, 51.

the borderlands of the Ukraine and the Crimea because Friar John and other missionaries of this epoch recall having seen some Europeans at the Tartar court and found that for the most part they were forcibly detained as artisans or slaves. But they never mention having met any European trader, who either resided there or who had ventured temporarily that far. It can therefore be presumed that the members of the Polo family really were the first Western merchants to be received as guests at those courts, in the same way that Friar John was the first Latin to come into direct contact with the Tartars in their own empire.

Since the missions " ad Tartaros " were a Christian enterprise entrusted to the mendicant orders, it was natural that the zeal of the missionaries and their spirit of sacrifice and adventure should not remain circumscribed by one area. When, a few months after the departure of Friar John, the Council of Lyons decreed that such missions were to be considered an international undertaking and a duty, they soon increased and multiplied, rivalling one another in abnegation and fervor. Though the practical fruit of their labours was small, these enterprises opened up new ways and wider horizons towards the further exploration of Asia. The first to take advantage of them, a few years later, was the French-Flemish Minorite Friar William of Rubruk, an emulator of Friar John whose account he had read before starting on his journey to the Tartar capital.[31]

* * *

Terrible as were the dangers and trials of such a journey, the experience of Friar John had shown that, with proper credentials, one might travel through Tartar territory with the relative certainty of not being put

[31] *Ibid.*, pp. 150, and 213.

to death. The respect of the barbarians for the dignity of an ambassador was such that, in his letter of reply to the Pope, which Friar John was commissioned to carry, the Grand Khan Küyük justified the outrages committed in Christian Europe during the Mongolian incursions by citing the fact that Tartar emissaries had been killed when sent to the West.[32] Hence the Pope's legate, although he might be treated haughtily and suspiciously, was nevertheless in a privileged position, and his person was to a certain extent inviolate. William of Rubruk, a simple missionary, was far from possessing this high dignity, although he was protected by a letter of recommendation from Louis IX, the king of France, to the Tartar prince Sartach, ruler of the Western borderlands of the Mongolian empire.

The risk of being treated as a spy or as a trouble-maker was far greater for him. Mongolian authorities were at that time particularly justified in being suspicious of Christian churchmen travelling within their territories without official credentials. A year before Friar William's departure, a clerk from Accon, who made believe that he was a subject of the King of France, reached the court of Mangu Khan and was sent back as an ambassador to the Pope. But he was arrested and thrown into prison by order of the Emperor of Nicaea who sent back to Mangu, as a warning and as an act of courtesy, the " Golden Tablet " which confirmed the high dignity conferred by the Mongolian emperor on this impostor.[33] But after the first successful contact between the Roman Curia and the Mongols, Tartar embassies to the Pope and to the King of France

[32] *Ibid.*, p. 141.
[33] The story of this man who wished to cheat the Pope as he had cheated the Tartar Emperor, is told by William himself, *Sinica francisc.*, p. 255; Rockhill, *The Journey*, p. 181.

became more frequent and, later on, even habitual, thus rendering ever safer and more inviting, so to speak, further exploration into remotest Asia. And this is not one of the least of the glories which adorn the history of the Order of St. Francis.

In the years following the return of Friar John, various Tartar embassies came to the King of France, who was then in the Levant, and to the Pope. On his side, Innocent IV sent several Dominicans to the commanders of the Tartar armies in Asia Minor, among whom were Friar Ascelin and Simon of St. Quentin.[34] King Louis IX sent his first mission in charge of Friar Andrew of Longjumeau, a Dominican, who had already been in contact with Mongol dignitaries in western Asia. He reached the Mongol court after the death of Küyük Khan and when his widow Ogul Gaimish was Empress-Regent.[35] Only fragments of the reports of these missionaries have been preserved to us and then indirectly, in the *Speculum Historiale* of Vincent of Beauvais, so that we can recognize only superficially their intellectual character and establish the degree of the acquaintance which these men had with Asia and its peoples.[36]

But undoubtedly these Dominicans are much more inclined to believe and to tell fables or strange stories

[34] For these missions to the Mongols, cf. B. Altaner, *The Dominikane-missionen*, etc., especially Ch. VI, p. 116 *et seq.*, from which it appears that the Dominicans prevailed in Eastern Europe, while it is certain that the Franciscans were preponderant in Central Asia and in the Far East. No details have been handed down about the journey of the Franciscan monk Gerard of Prato, a scholar of some repute in his day, who went " ad Tartaros " and is called by Salimbene " Lector Tusciae " (*op. cit.*, p. 210).

[35] The principal details of his report are related in Rockhill's introductory notice to *The Journey*, etc., p. xxiv-xxxv with particular emphasis on the information William of Rubruck got from this Dominican friar.

[36] *Speculum Historiale*, Douai, 1624, Vol. VI, Chap. XXXI *et seq.*

than the contemporary Franciscan missionaries.[37] Thus Friar Andrew surrounded his information about the Mongols with mystery and fantastic details, and made believe that the Tartars came from a great sandy desert situated at the Eastern end of the world near some marvellous impassable mountains behind which were confined the people of Gog and Magog. Furthermore he related that the first great chief of the Mongols was miraculously converted to Christianity and that God promised him in a vision dominion over Prester John. The Friar adapted much of his experience and knowledge of Asia to the common image and to the dominating conceptions of his age. It is undeniable that, in this way, these Dominicans are responsible for having unanimously confirmed the reports, spread abroad by the Tartars for political purposes, of the conversion to Christianity of the chief Mongol sovereigns.

It was with this vision in mind that the holy King Louis IX charged the Franciscan Friar William of Rubruk to instruct these chieftains of the East in the doctrines of the true faith. William set out from Cyprus in March 1253, accompanied by Friar Bartholomew of Cremona, another Minorite. Stopping at Constantinople and at Soldaia, the emporium of the Crimea, they then proceeded slowly as far as the encampment of Sartach, the son of Batu, who commanded the frontier regions of Tartary and whose horde was at that time at a distance of three day's march this side of the Volga. The two friars arrived at this encampment on July 31st. This was the goal assigned them by the King who

---

[37] This may be inferred not only from the report of Friar Andrew but from the accounts of other Dominicans, as e. g. Jordanus Catalani de Severac whose *Mirabilia* is more a collection of fables than of personal experiences and observations (cf. the edition of *Les Merveilles de l'Asie* by H. Cordier, Paris, 1920).

counted on the conversion and the ultimate assistance of this Tartar ruler. But Sartach was only superficially interested in this religious mission which had come to his territory empty-handed except for many vestments and sacred objects and a case full of books of devotion—even though some of them were richly adorned with miniatures.

It seemed to Friar William that the Tartar chieftain was more inclined to ridicule the Christians than to profess the same faith as they did.[38] In order to get rid of him as soon as possible, and in the most polite way, Sartach induced him to proceed to Batu, Khan of Kipchak or Western Tartary, who in return despatched him a few days later, in the company of a rich and insolent Mongolian personage, to the Grand Khan Mangu, then living at Karakorum, the capital of Mongolia. Evidently the provincial rulers of the Western borderlands were convinced that the monk was able to give valuable information about the political and military situation in the Near East where Tartar expansion interfered with the French sphere of interests.

To reach Karakorum from Batu's camp meant a four months' journey on horseback through unknown lands toward an uncertain destination, which the Tartar dignitary took pains to describe in darkest terms, with the intention either of putting him to the test or of dissuading him from proceeding further. Having left the horde of Batu on September 16th, the intrepid monk arrived at the horde of Mangu on December 27th and was permitted to stay there until Palm Sunday 1254, when he entered the capital with the emperor's court. Here he was allowed to remain until the middle of August.

The city of Karakorum, originally the camp of Ong-

[38] *Sinica francisc.*, p. 209; Rockhill, p. 116.

Khan, the Christian Kerait, and once a military center of Genghis Khan, was the first political and administrative nucleus of the Mongolian empire and also the earliest municipal settlement established by these city-destroying nomads.[39] Just as Friar John had sketched an authentic and graphic description of a characteristic Tartar city of tents, so Friar William traced a vivid and detailed picture of this budding capital situated on the plain bordering the upper course of the Orkhon in the heart of Mongolia and of the empire. Friar William, who measured the world with the spirit and eye of a Parisian, was very much disappointed with Karakorum which, he said, " is not as important as Bourg St. Denis," that is, as the famous suburb of Paris. He adds that the abbey of St. Denis, the royal residence of the Capetian dynasty, was worth ten times more than the palace of the Grand Khan.

The city had two sections: that of the Saracens with many and oft-frequented markets, and that of the Chinese " who are all artisans." [40] Beyond these quarters rose the great palaces of the functionaries, the twelve temples erected to the idols of the twelve regions of the Empire, two mosques, and, " at the city borders," the Christian church. The capital was enclosed and defended by a wall having gates at the four cardinal points; near each were markets, specializing, respectively, in cereals, small animals, cattle and carts, and horses. The palace of the Grand Khan, with its large and sumptuous ceremonial hall, its various buildings

[39] An ample description of the capital in Marco Polo, *The Book*, etc., I, p. 225 *et seq.* Bibliography in *Sinica francisc.*, p. 30, n. 3. Friar William's description *ibid.*, p. 285 *et seq.* and Rockhill, *The Journey*, etc., p. 220.

[40] Speaking of the Kytaians, Friar John asserted that " there are no better craftsmen in the world in everything they work." *Sinica francisc.*, p. 58.

used for keeping provisions and the Imperial treasure,
rose outside the walls in proximity to the city.

This brief description of the seat of the Grand Khan
is a rare bit of testimony and a masterpiece of precision
and vivacity, especially remarkable because it has
hardly its equal in mediaeval literature and is surpassed
only by Marco Polo's excellent picture of the city of
Khanbaliq.[41] There is extraordinary variety in William's portrayal of the environment and different
aspects of the court and of public and private life,
which he describes in his picturesque gallicised Latin.
In this great caravanserai there were many Christians,
nearly all of whom belonged to the Greek rite or to the
Nestorian sect. Western civilisation was represented by
a woman from Lorraine, the wife of a Ruthenian who
worked, apparently with success, as an architect;
furthermore by a nephew of the Bishop of Belleville in
Normandy, and finally by William Bucher, a French
goldsmith, so that Friar William had the welcome surprise of finding a little colony of fellow-countrymen
in that far-off land, people who furnished him with
precious information on all customs of the East and
who made his stay more agreeable by facilitating and
encouraging his mission.

These few Latins, were the only fixed representatives
of the Western civilisation in that Asiatic world whose
fleeting contacts with Europe were almost exclusively
political and warlike. They were not there of their own

---

[41] Marco Polo, *The Book*, etc., I, p. 374 *et seq*. Generally, in mediaeval
descriptions of towns and monuments, the poetic, fabulous and legendary
elements prevail over the realistic traits, as can be seen in the *Mirabilia
Urbis Romae*, in the descriptions of Constantinople, Paris, Venice, Milan
etc. and in that of Quinsay by Marco Polo himself (cf. the author's *Storia
Letteraria delle Scoperte geografiche*, p. 107 *et seq*.). An Armenian
description of Paris (cf. *Revue des Études Armeniennes*, Vol. XI (1931-
33), p. 1 *et seq*.) reveals the same tendency in Oriental literatures.

accord. When the Tartars exterminated the populations of the cities which they conquered, they sometimes spared the lives of persons whom they thought could be of signal use, taking them along as prisoners. Thus it was that the missionaries, and later Marco Polo, found in the entourage of the Grand Khan, besides a number of Slavs and Hungarians, also a few Germans, Frenchmen and Englishmen, or some descendants of these Westerners scattered throughout those vast Asiatic populations.

According to what Brother William gives us to understand, the Mongolians had no architects.[42] The goldsmith Bucher was also an engineer, as was quite usual at that time for one of his profession. The Tartars had taken him captive at Belgrade, where he worked, and dragged him to Karakorum. There he fashioned for them those mechanized contrivances and the works of his art which the Friar has minutely described for us.[43] This was the type of work which the Mongolian sovereigns held in highest esteem. At that time engineering was for those Asiatic nations the most characteristic expression of the Western civilisation. Technology was only slightly known in the East and was entirely unknown to the Mongolian peoples. While the Chinese were admirable artisans, they had little notion of mechanical engineering, either as an art or as a science.

[42] Speaking of a Ruthenian who married a French woman and lived at Karakorum, the Friar affirms that " he knew how to make houses, a very good trade among them " (*Sinica francisc.*, p. 253). Rockhill supposed that this architect probably constructed tent-frames, " for all the houses at Karakorum were made by the Chinese " (*The Journey*, etc., p. 177 n. 1), but the Byzantine influence was certainly represented in this rapidly growing capital, during the epoch in which the Tartars began to adapt themselves to a sort of urban civilisation, and employed for this purpose not only Chinese artisans but also occidental artists and craftsmen.

[43] *Sinica francisc.*, p. 276 *et seq.*; Rockhill, p. 208.

5

Marco Polo could say of them that they were skillful craftsmen, wise merchants and " good natural philoso- phers," but when it came to conquering " Saianfu," which the troops of the Grand Khan had been besieging for three years, Niccolò, Maffeo and Marco Polo en- trusted to a German and to a Nestorian the building of powerful war-machines of their own invention which, by hurling great stones into the city, made the popula- tion decide to surrender. " Et as Tartars senbloit la greignor merveille dou monde." [44]

It is well known that the success of the Jesuit mis- sionaries of the sixteenth and seventeenth centuries in China was due, to a large extent, to the marvellous mechanical objects, such as clocks, fountains and animated statues, which they constructed for the diver- sion of the Emperors or for public utility—things, in fact, differing little from those which had already proved the delight of the Tartar monarchs. The Tartars certainly appreciated in the Latins more the versatility of their talents and their practical ability than their religious doctrines and morality. Thus the Grand Khan himself gave William of Rubruk to understand at his farewell audience, warning him that their own faith was sufficient and adequate to enable them to live in peace, if not with men, at least with God. [45]

This same opinion was held by the Nestorians, Saracens, Buddhists, Taoists, Lamaists, Manichaeans and Shamanists with whom the Friar came in contact during his stay, and among whom and among whose

---

[44] Marco Polo, *Il Milione*, p. 139. A description of those military engines in Yule's comment to Marco Polo, *The Book*, etc., II, pp. 161-169. For the different versions of the text which make this passage difficult to clarify in all its details, cf. the notes to Marco Polo, *Description*, etc., p. 317 *et seq.*

[45] *Sinica francisc.*, p. 297 *et seq.*; Rockhill, *op. cit.*, p. 235 *et seq.*

doctrines—although he argued with them, or gathered information from others, or visited in their temples— he was able to distinguish little and to understand even less. Instead, it appeared quite clear to him that his mission was a failure, despite the six baptisms he had administered, and that the conversion of the Mongol sovereigns which he had hoped for was a snare and a delusion. Those who profited most from this expedition were the few Catholic residents of Karakorum, in as much as Brother Bartholomew, not having the heart to undertake the return journey, settled permanently among them, and let Friar William return home alone.

For the King of France this mission was another humiliating disappointment.[46] If his feeling was justified from a political and religious point of view, nevertheless we owe to this enterprise one of the most interesting and original works of mediaeval literature, which, in its completeness and in the reliability of its geographical, historical and ethnological information, vies with the *Historia Mongalorum* of Friar John and with the *Milione* of Marco Polo. Though Friar William's account differs from the one and the other in many respects, yet it shares with them both a fundamental and sometimes a decisive affinity.

But it is just this affinity which reveals the difference in the character, mind and culture of the travellers. The predominantly religious objective of his journey directed the attention of Friar William especially toward the different aspects of the Asiatic creeds which had been entirely ignored or radically misunderstood in the Western world. Although he did not even try to penetrate the spiritual and doctrinal substance of these religions and

[46] The first had been the failure of the mission entrusted to Andrew of Lonjumeau. Cf. Rockhill, *op. cit.* p. 31.

considered them as monstrous aberrations inspired by the devil, nevertheless he gave a vivid and reliable description of their temples and rites, revealing for the first time some characteristic external aspects of Buddhism and Lamaism; he described the magic rites and superstitions of the Nestorians, and contributed many items of information to the knowledge of exorcism as practised by Mongolian Shamanists. His description of his public discussions with the priests of all these creeds has no parallel in the mediaeval literature of travel. No chronicle or account of contemporary events contains an episode comparable in richness of details or in suggestive expressiveness to the report of the audiences granted to him by the emperor.

All these sections of his book are well known and have been highly appreciated by historians and folklore specialists. His contributions to geography have been emphasized many times and commented upon. In fact, the general view he had of the physical geography, the ethnological variations and the general conditions of the Asiatic continent was much more comprehensive, extended and detailed than the narrative sketched by his predecessor. But there are still more angles to William's report and to his personality that deserve closer attention and merit a more exhaustive estimate of their interest and value. This keen observer of men and of facts was more sensitive to natural scenery than any other traveller of his epoch. He admired the " most beautiful wood growing on a plain full of fountains and rivulets " situated in the Northern part of the Crimea, and was impressed by the country between the Don and the Volga.[47] The vast plain of the Lake Ala-Kul, surrounded by high mountains and irrigated by innumerable streams inspired in him a word of admira-

---

[47] *Sinica francisc.*, p. 198; Rockhill, p. 99.

tion.[48] These expressions revealing the personal reaction
of the friar to the landscape of Asia are scanty enough
and limited to a single word. But even such words are
very rare in mediaeval descriptive and narrative literature. His interest in the natural aspects of the regions
which he had visited is indirectly expressed by frequent
and sometimes extended or detailed descriptions which
are even scarcer or perhaps non-existent in contemporary books of geography and even of travel.[49]

The Friar's indifference towards vegetation appears
from the fact that there is no tree or plant mentioned
in his extensive and varied report. As we have seen
already, this is a characteristic mediaeval attitude which
has its symptomatic expression in the very conventional
and distorted shapes of trees and plants in contemporary artistic representations. On the other hand, an
excellent description of the Siberian oxen, the famous
yaks which drew the big dwellings of the Mongols,
reflects the typical mediaeval realism in representing
and sketching animals. The correct enumeration of the
distinguishing marks of this bovine species mentions
the " very hairy tails like horses . . . , bellies and backs
covered with hair. They are lower on their legs than
other oxen, but much stronger . . . and have slender,
long, curved horns, so sharp that it is always necessary
to cut off their points." The item that " the cows will
not let themselves be milked unless sung to," belongs to
the many anecdotal features of mediaeval zoology, as
does the story that if they see a man dressed in red,
these oxen throw themselves on him to kill him.[50]

* * *

[48] *Ibid.*, p. 225, 140 respectively.
[49] William's principal contributions to geography, natural history,
ethnology, anthropology, history of religions, etc., are enumerated by
Rockhill, *The Journey*, etc., Introduction, p. xxxvii *et seq.*
[50] *Sinica francisc.*, p. 233 *et seq.*; Rockhill, *op. cit.*, p. 151.

Friar William departed from Karakorum on the
fifteenth of August 1254. For three weeks, always
travelling westward, he followed the envoys of an In-
dian " sultan " probably on the route to Turkestan,
but he failed to tell us what he heard from them about
their own country. About one month later he arrived
at the encampment of Batu on the Volga; thence he
proceeded by way of the Caucasus, Armenia Major and
Asia Minor to Iconium, the modern Konia, then the
capital of a Seljuk sultanate.[51] There, after many in-
cidents, he first encountered Latins: several Frenchmen
and the Italian merchants, Niccoló di San Siro, a
Geonese, and Bonifacio da Molendino, a Venetian. The
latter had, between them, monopolized the trade in
alum.[52] These merchants took pains to direct Friar
William towards the Armenian port of Curca, in Christian territory where, on May 5, 1255, he once more saw
the Mediterranean. But on arriving he found that his
king had returned to France, and that a decree of the
Capitular Fathers of Antioch had assigned to him the
residence of Accon, thus preventing him from returning
to Paris. To this decision, not entirely comprehensible,
considering the importance of Friar William's mission,
we owe the detailed and ample itinerary which he wrote
out in letter form and addressed to Saint Louis.[53]

The character of this extraordinary document shows

[51] The chronology of William's journey in Rockhill's introduction, p.
xlv *et seq.*

[52] On the commercial specialities of the Italians in Asia Minor useful
indications can be found in the works already referred to by Heyd (cf.
supra, p. 3 n. 5) and Schaube (p. 6 n. 12). For the trade routes in
that region, see C. R. Beazley, *The Dawn of Modern Geography*, Vol.
II, p. 456 *et seq.*

[53] Probably the fathers intended to benefit by William's extraordinary
experiences for their own missionary activities. Later on the Friar was
allowed to join King Louis IX in Paris. Cf. Rockhill, *The Journey*,
etc., p. xxxix.

it to have been an improvisation. Whatever is lacking
in it of the almost scientific orderliness of Friar John's
report is amply compensated for by the vivacity of Friar
William's narrative, by his tendency to rhapsodize and
to quote anecdotes, and by the variety and richness of
the subjects of which he treats and his reflections upon
them. Friar William sees and describes things with the
superiority and breadth of view of a cultivated man
who quotes his Virgil from memory, corrects the writings
of Isidore, completes those of Solinus, is mindful of the
chronicles, and couples with his knowledge the advantages of a natural acumen and a critical spirit. He is
constantly on the alert to know the reasons for things.
In fact, this desire is to him a necessity, and his curiosity
extends far beyond the limits of his mission, so much
so that, to the geographical and ethnological notions
about Asia and its history, he adds minute descriptions of customs, of household furnishings, of foods and
drinks, of the ceremonials he witnessed, of rites, of
money and of every aspect of the life of the inhabitants
with whom he came in contact. His account gives the
first reports—and amazing ones they are—concerning
the artistic tastes, the public worship and prejudices,
the languages and handwriting, and the commercial
usages among these Oriental peoples.

His residence in the capital of that vast and varied
Empire revealed to Brother William's observing and
penetrating gaze the most mixed and exotic setting then
in existence. From this center a far-reaching view was
ensured, a mine of information was available for ac-
quainting him with the complicated structure of this
Eastern world. The impression he received was so lively
and lasting, so multifarious and plastic, that once he

lamented not knowing how to paint so that he might be able to portray more clearly all that he had seen.[54]

His notable gifts as a writer are apparent in the personal touches in this itinerary, written in fluent and simple even if barbarous Latin. His free and lively style at times betrays a gentle humor, but again it shows a strong and ill-concealed rebelliousness. It can rise to dramatic heights, as when he relates his theological discussions; or to the plastic qualities of a relief, as in the description of his audiences with the Grand Khan; or to a pathetic solemnity, as when he tells of his parting in tears with William Bucher, the goldsmith, who, amid the emotion of farewells, has a touching thought for his holy King.[55] With all this our friar does not fail to give us the precise information, the lengthy enumerations and the concise, characteristic details in which the book abounds.[56] With this account the image of Asia definitely emerges from the realm of fancy and conjecture and becomes in every respect a positive and lasting acquisition of European culture.[57]

William of Rubruk was able to extend his knowledge eastward because of the frequent contacts which he, as the first European, had with men of Chinese origin living in Karakorum. Even if these men, perhaps intentionally, led him to believe some fables and stories, we still owe to him the first notice of paper money, intro-

[54] *Sinica francisc.*, p. 173. This expression is most remarkable for that age when painting did not attempt to represent nature realistically.

[55] These episodes in *Sinica francisc.*, pp. 289-300 and 311 *et seq.*; Rockhill, *The Journey*, etc., pp. 226-239 and p. 254.

[56] Like all mediaeval travellers, Friar William is inaccurate in his statements of distances with the characteristic tendency toward exaggeration. Examples in *Sinica francisc.*, p. 165 and 220.

[57] The first, and only, mediaeval author who recognized the importance of Friar William's report was Roger Bacon who read it thoroughly and discussed it with the author in Paris and later embodied in his *Opus Majus* every geographical detail. Cf. Rockhill, *op. cit.*, p. xxxix.

duced into China in the ninth century of our era and
later adopted on a grand scale by the Mongols throughout the Empire. He was the first to identify the
Chinese with the Seres of antiquity and described
" these Cathayans as small men, who in speaking
aspirate strongly through the nose, and in common with
all Orientals, have small openings of the eyes." [58] He
admired their silken garments and their skill in dyeing
them, their artistic ability, their talent for medicine,
and their manner of writing "with a brush such as
painters paint with." [59] From him we learn that Prester
John is a legendary Nestorian figure originating in an
historical Christian monarch not unlike the Asiatic
sovereign whom Marco Polo identifies and records.

As more effective knowledge of these countries increased, the old fables shifted and assumed new shapes.
Through the Friar's knowledge of the old tales of wonder concerning those regions and of the wide-spread
teratology of antique origin he was prepared to accept
as authentic the Chinese stories of the golden walls of
Si-ngan-fu or of certain creatures, a cubit high and hairy
all over, which dwell in inaccessible holes in the rocks
of the eastern parts of Cathay and get along by some
kind of jumping motion because they are not able to
bend their knees.[60]

In the two reports of the Franciscan missionaries we
find the first mention of Tibet, of which Marco Polo
later records such strange things. But in spite of all the
evil Marco Polo recounts of the Tibetans in his description of their abject customs, he does not represent them
as ferocious as does Friar William, who says they are
cannibals that devour their parents and afterwards use

[58] *Sinica francisc.*, p. 236; Rockhill, p. 155.
[59] *Ibid.*, pp. 271, 201-02, respectively.
[60] *Ibid.*, pp. 269 *et seq.*, 199, respectively.

their skulls as receptacles from which they drink merrily to their memory.[61] Perhaps there is concealed under this tale a vague reminiscence of the Tibetan tablets composed of earth and human ashes, called *ts'a ts'a,* and used all over the country as objects of religious worship.[62] But in any case both friars have evidently located in Tibet the legend of Gog and Magog, these famous cannibalistic peoples who were relegated to the farthest East in the poems and doctrinal treatises which formed a part of the general culture of the thirteenth century. At least the information gathered by Friar William at Karakorum seemed to confirm the ghastly stories told about these distant peoples by ancient and mediaeval authors.[63] The two friars doubtless had in

[61] *Ibid.,* pp. 234, 151, respectively. A similar story is told by Friar John (*Sinica francisc.,* pp. 60-61) about the people of Buri-Thabet, not yet satisfactorily identified, and supposed to be Tibet proper or the borderlands of Tsaidan or Sining. The region of Tibor mentioned by Odoric of Pordenone in his *Relatio* (*Sinica francisc.,* p. 484 *et seq.*) and the Tebet of Marco Polo (*The Book,* etc., II, pp. 42-53) correspond with the present Tibet, but it is doubtful that these travellers visited the country. The bibliography for this difficult discussion is given by P. van den Wyngaert, *Sinica francisc.,* p. lxxxi, n. 6. Some sort of cannibalism is attributed to the Tibetans or the Kashmirians, or even to the Tartars, by Marco Polo, *The Book,* etc., I, p. 301 and Yule's n. 9, p. 311 *et seq.* The charge of cannibalism is made against the Mongols by Friar John (*Sinica francisc.,* p. 47) and occasionally by Friar William (*ibid.,* p. 171; Rockhill, *The Journey,* etc., p. 63, n. 3).

[62] Cf. G. Tucci, in *Indo-Tibetica,* I, Roma, 1932. These *ts'a ts'a* represent the only somewhat macabre aspect of Lamaistic worship which has no direct connection with the details related by the mediaeval travellers.

[63] The hints of Asiatic cannibalism are suspicious for the reason that it is spoken of, in very particular terms, in earlier texts of a literary tradition anterior to all these travel accounts and independent of them. Thus in one of the oldest versions of the *Letter of Prester John,* written before 1221, reference is made to the peoples relegated to the ends of Asia who " feed themselves with human flesh as well as with the meat of abortive animals," adding what the two friars relate independently of one another that " they avidly eat their parents as well as strangers,

mind what Pliny and Pomponius Mela told about the existence of anthropophagic peoples in the interior of Asia, a traditional assumption barely justified by actual experiences or by reliable witnesses from those places.

Likewise Friar William took pains to inform himself on the nature of the fabulous monsters of Asia, a matter belonging to the self-same cycle of information and notions. Indeed, when he was assured by a Chinese priest that no one had ever seen such beings, he was much surprised and doubted rather the sincerity of his informers that the reliability of such ancient teachings.[64] Thus the stories of cannibalism were one of the inevitable elements of every actual or imaginary picture of Asia. No mediaeval traveller, up to the time of Christopher Columbus and even after him, had ever refrained from telling similar tales of cannibalism, reference to which was not alone a commonplace in this sort of literature but always a source of excited popular curiosity.[65]

saying that it is a very sacred thing to eat human flesh." The names of those peoples are: Gog and Magog, Amic, Agic, etc." (cf. Zarncke, *Der Presbyter Johannes*, p. 911). This story is repeated more or less completely in the popular treatises of the XIIIth century, e. g. in the *Mappemonde* by a certain Pierre (Ch. V. Langlois, *op. cit.*, p. 128) and by the well known *Image du Monde* (*ibid.*, p. 168). Marco Polo (*The Book*, etc., II, p. 264) describes this form of anthropophagy as a custom prevailing in the Sunda Islands. All those stories of a presumed widespread Asiatic cannibalism were propagated through the legends of Alexander the Great in connection with Gog and Magog (cf. A. R. Anderson, *Gog and Magog, Alexander's Gate*, etc., Cambridge, Mass., 1932) and they were confirmed by Pomponius Mela and other antique geographers known in the Middle Ages. The problem has been studied recently by A. Hermann, *Das Land der Seide und Tibet im Lichte der Antike*, Leipzig, 1938, p. 32 *et seq.* and p. 125. Texts in R. Hennig's *Terrae Incognitae*.

[64] *Sinica francisc.*, p. 259; Rockhill, *The Journey*, etc., p. 198 *et seq.*

[65] For the numerous hints at Asiatic cannibalism, cf. the Index to Yule's edition of Marco Polo, *The Book*, etc., and R. Hennig, *Terrae Incognitae*, IV, p. 30 etc.

However, as is evident, the fundamental ideas of learned and poetic tradition became ever more slender and diaphanous when compared with the reality as viewed by these missionaries in a spirit of independence. Many things, especially of a spiritual and religious nature, they barely noticed or altogether misunderstood, but their judgment is never at fault when they treat of the concrete expressions of those exotic civilisations and the peculiar features of the life of semi-barbarous nomads. Certainly this judgment is not marked by benevolence. Although Sartach, Batu and even Mangu Khan, the all-powerful emperor, were always very polite, helpful and affable to him, Friar William was so vexed by their political arrogance and tribal presumption that—if it were allowed to him, as he said—he " would preach war against them throughout the world and with all his energy." [66] He was disgusted by everything connected with their methods of conquest and expansion, especially stigmatizing their customary ruse of making a treacherous peace with the countries that they wanted to subjugate or to destroy.[67]

Contrary to Marco Polo, who always speaks with sympathy and deference of things pertaining to the Tartars, these friars, while remaining objective and outwardly impassive, are still more or less openly inspired by continual resentment and contempt for this barbarous and strange world. The Venetian traveller never dares to express a word of criticism or to sound unfavorable to the policy and the renown of the Tartar rulers. He was a boy when he left his country and was transformed into an Oriental by the many years of intercourse with Asiatic peoples. He became a func-

---

[66] *Sinica francisc.*, p. 244; Rockhill, *The Journey*, p. 167.
[67] *Ibid.*, pp. 290, 226, respectively.

tionary of the Grand Khan at an epoch when the court
and the culture of the Mongolian rulers had almost
assumed the ancient traditions of China and its higher
civilisation. The period of Kubilai Khan marked the
apex of Tartar power. The grandiose and varied, the
picturesque and spectacular appearance of Peking and
other Chinese cities, must have filled the Venetian new-
comer with admiration and surprise, and aroused in the
traveller coming from Europe many reflections when
he beheld the splendor with an intelligent spirit and
sound judgment. The friars who had reached the heart
of Asia toward the middle of the thirteenth century with
the intention of evangelizing it, of establishing an
apostolate and of making converts, recognized the
futility of their hopes and labors in the midst of the
unstable, artificial and always excitable atmosphere of
these Tartar hordes. This being the case, they certainly
were not inclined to write of them in a serene spirit.
Friar John of Pian del Càrpine had advanced toward
Asia, passing by the skeletons and skulls of the human
victims of Tartar invasions of Russia; and Brother
William had in mind the memory of his Polish and
Hungarian confrères massacred by the hordes of that
same Batu to whom he was obliged to pay homage.
All the more admirable, therefore, is the objectivity of
their judgment, the calmness of their impressions and
the penetration of their criticisms. Still more to be
admired is the self-control they exercised in submitting
themselves " for the greater glory of God " to the
humiliating ceremony of Genghiskhanid sovereigns, by
appearing barefooted and bending the knee before them,
and by suffering with dignity and patience the vexations
inflicted upon them by functionaries, and the threats
of the evil-minded. It should also be remembered that
they were ever conscious of the fate which might befall

them, being, as they were, quite defenseless and at the mercy of an invincible tyrant.

The conciliatory and accommodating attitude of the Franciscans contrasts with that of the Dominican missionaries who arrived in 1247 at the camp of Baachu, the Tartar commander in Persia.[68] They not only refused to submit to the humiliating court ceremony, but they assumed and maintained toward that prince a rashly haughty attitude which was considered provocative and which, in the end, jeopardized the whole mission.

We may recognize in the different attitudes of the Franciscans and the Dominicans, under precisely the same circumstances, expressions of the respective characters of the two Orders as Dante saw them: the one " seraphic in his ardor " and the other " benign to his own and to his enemies harsh." [69] It is best to leave this problem to hypothesis, but in order to weigh its import it will be sufficient to compare the methods adopted, respectively, by the Franciscans, the Dominicans and the Jesuits during the period of the renewed activity of these missions in the sixteenth century. In that case it will not be difficult to ascribe the different aspects and effects of the missions to the respective characteristic spiritual constitutions of each Order, though all of them have the same end in view. Granting this, it may at least be established that these more active, cultivated and intelligent friars were not content

[68] The details of this mission are related by B. Altaner, *Die Dominikanemissionen*, p. 124 *et seq.* and discussed *ibid.*, p. 225 *et seq.* Also by P. Pelliot, *Les Mongols et la Papauté, passim* and G. Soranzo, *Il Papato, l'Europa Cristiana e i Tartari*, Cap. VI. A short survey of the principal episodes and results is given by Rockhill, *The Journey*, etc., p. xxiv *et seq.* About Baachu, *ibid.*, p. 265.

[69] *Paradiso*, XI, v. 36, XII, v. 57, respectively.

merely to comply with the rules of their Orders, but, adapting themselves to circumstances, were inspired by the examples set them by their founders. It seems, in fact, that in their work of religious and political propagandizing among the Tartars, the Dominicans proceeded with a fanatical impetus, passionately proclaiming Christian doctrine, much in the same way as, a few decades later, Raymond Lull conducted his missionary and literary activities among the Moslems of Africa; whereas one seems to recognize in the attitude of the Franciscans sent out to Asia the influence of St. Francis himself whose example they tirelessly followed, with enlightened compassion for living creatures, and with no harshness against dissenting people. The attitude of St. Francis in his discussions with the Sultan of Egypt near Damietta was exemplary for his followers. They relied for the success of their missions on a patience that was not resignation, rather than on dialectics that admitted of no concessions. These Franciscans accepted (while secretly protesting but with the spirit of hope for the future) the world as they found it, with all its human experiences; the Dominicans instead tended to acquire more rapid and tangible successes even at the cost of immediate struggles or, as in the cases cited, of open scandal. Hence they were less adapted than others to deal with the Oriental character and to comply with its more or less justifiable requirements.

However, in these first attempts, neither of the two methods led to tangible results. But now at last serious-minded and responsible people of the West had documents of sufficient validity to enable them to organize more prudently every similar enterprise, and to provide them with exact notions of almost every aspect of the mysterious Asiatic continent and of the geographical distribution of its peoples. When one con-

siders under what conditions, seventy years earlier, the
legate of Alexander III had set out in search of Prester
John, one can realize the extent and depth of the reliable
information acquired in so short a time.

But on what does their importance depend? or to
what witnesses can be ascribed the abundance of data,
notices and details supplied by the two friars in their
comprehensive reports? This question allows us to raise
the question, to which we cannot be indifferent, of what
value should be attributed to this geographical literature
which arose in the thirteenth century out of the experiences of a few intrepid and intelligent explorers.

In the prologue of his book Marco Polo tells us that,
" thinking it almost impossible ever to leave the service
of the great Kaan, king of the Tartars, I only wrote a
few small things in my notebooks." [70] This certainly
was not the method followed by his precursors, although, of course, they knew that they had to report
what they had heard and observed during their stay
and journeys in Asia. Friar John seems to have written
the *Historia Mongalorum* while still on his travels,
probably in Russia where he tarried a while on his
return journey.[71] Friar William wrote his *Itinerary* at
Accon, immediately upon his arrival, to serve as a tem-
porary piece of information for his King while he was
awaiting the opportunity of giving him personally the
details of his journey—as later he did. It is certain that
neither of the two missionaries used notes and that both
wrote their accounts relying only on their memory, just
as Marco Polo did when he dictated his work to Rustician " in that same dungeon at Genoa," while the
recollection of their adventures was still fresh.[72]

[70] The passage is only in Ramusio's version (cf. Marco Polo, *Il Milione*,
p. 4 n. and *Description of the World*, p. 73).

[71] *Sinica francisc.*, p. 8.

[72] Cf. *Il Milione* ed. by Foscolo Benedetto, p. 4, note b.

It was not a mediaeval custom to make preliminary notes with a view to writing afterwards a more complete record of personal experiences. We moderns have no adequate idea of the power and extent of the memory of the men of those times. The drawing up of any sort of preparatory notes on the part of these travellers, may at once be dismissed as a superfluous act, for their minds easily retained the memory of foreign things, of dates, and even of difficult, strange and unaccustomed names. Even fleeting impressions and details of small importance were kept unaltered in their recollections more or less clearly and lastingly, according to their capacity for observation and the liveliness of their interest.

What these first explorers of Asia lacked was neither the retentiveness of memory nor the power of observation, but essentially the aptitude for organizing their impressions and of giving a coherent account of their experiences. This inability to reduce empirical attainments to systematic order is very characteristic of the mediaeval way of thinking. While Marco Polo transformed his reminiscences of travel into an intentionally objective description of the world, the accounts of his precursors still bear the mark of personal narratives combining in a promiscuous style the realistic image of the things observed with the discreet expression of their personal reactions.

There is a constant relation in their books between the things described from their own experience and those referred to on information received from others. In the first case both friars rely unhesitatingly on their own impressions. In the second, for the sake of prudence, they express some reserve—admirable in this, as much for their honesty, as for the tenacity and freshness of their memories. Their originality did not consist merely in the novelty of the things they related and described,

6

but also in the fact that the authors of these first travel-books of a new era had neither sources to consult nor models to follow. They portrayed, without rhetorical artifice and at the same time without excessive ingenuousness, the image living within them, to which they readily gave such expressions as they deemed adequate to the subject and sufficient for their purpose.

* * *

IV. THE ELDER POLOS

In the interval between the return of Friar William of Rubruk and the departure of Marco Polo from Venice, that is, between 1254 and 1271, we know of only one expedition from Europe for the Far East. We refer to the journey undertaken by Maffeo and Niccolò Polo, respectively the uncle and the father of Marco.[1] The information we have of this journey is rather vague and fragmentary. It is given in the prologue of the *Milione*, but with such paucity of facts that it seems as though a veil of mystery was drawn over the recollection of this great undertaking.[2] The vague hints, the laconic style and outline of this prologue form a remarkable contrast to the overflowing abundance, the infinite variety of material, and the extent of Marco Polo's recollections. This prologue may be compared to the slender prelude of a great and animated symphony. The small amount of positive information it holds is very well known and has been often related. But little attention has been paid, even by Colonel Yule and other commentators on Marco Polo's book, to these introductory chapters. This study of his precursors enables us to throw a fresh light upon the details of the expedition and to contribute new observations that will clarify both the events of the enterprise and its importance as a whole.

[1] The personal history of the travellers and the dates and circumstances of their journey are related by Yule's Introduction to Marco Polo, *The Book*, etc., I, pp. 13-26, and by Moule and Pelliot, Introduction to the *Description of the World*, I, p. 22 *et seq.*

[2] Marco Polo, *The Book*, etc., I, p. 1 *et seq.*; *Il Milione*, p. 3 *et seq.*; *The Description of the World*, p. 73 *et seq.*

When Maffeo and Niccolò Polo proceeded toward the interior of Asia, they had already lived for several years in the Levant, having taken up their abode, perhaps with their families, in Constantinople at the time of Baldwin II, the last Latin ruler of the Greek empire. It is certain that, during the absence of the two brothers, Niccolò's family was in Venice with young Marco, who had been born in 1254. We may presume that when his father and his uncle ventured into unknown lands, they knew that their absence would be a long one.

At Constantinople they must have engaged in various trades. But on moving to Soldaia in the Crimea, they specialized in commerce in precious stones. The port of Soldaia, on the Black Sea, was then the principal emporium for trading with Russia and the great Mongolian hinterland which was rapidly becoming more civilized and enriching itself ever more with new conquests. The Mongolian empire was at that time eager for merchandise and had extraordinary purchasing power. We may infer that the traffic in precious stones seemed to be particularly lucrative, not only because the Mongolian princes and their numerous women made a great display of them and collected them, but also because the introduction of paper money in many parts of the Empire added to their value and demand.

The Polos proved themselves really to be what Marco had called them, " wise and prudent," when they decided to abandon the decadent city of Constantinople— exhausted by wars and impoverished by sack and rapine. They tried their fortune among new peoples and more enterprising lords. While the geography of scholarly tradition, the popular treatises of cosmography and poetic imagination continued to describe the interior of Asia as the region that produces precious stones in an exhaustible abundance and variety, the two skill-

ful merchants gave up their customary commercial
enterprise and ventured into an immense and unexplored territory where they expected to do a good
stroke of business with a mere handful of jewels.

With this end in view, they decided to push on
beyond Soldaia toward the interior of Russia until they
arrived, with their jewels, at Sarai, on the Volga, the
seat of Berka, Khan of Kipchak, brother, and successor
of that Batu whom the missionaries had visited ten
years or more earlier. The two merchants, encouraged
by the good reception they received, remained a
year in the Khan's residences—that of Sarai to the
South, and Bolgara to the north. They probably
adapted themselves rapidly to the regular changes of
place, according to the seasons, characteristic of the
semi-nomadic population of this Tartar kingdom.

It is difficult to say in what kind of business the two
Venetians were engaged during their stay in this widely
extended but unproductive country of steppes and
woods. They had little in common, indeed, with its
poverty-stricken population of cattle-drivers and fur-
trappers. Nevertheless it is possible to recognize the
circumstances which decided the two Polos to defer
their homeward journey to carry home the profits of
their trade.

In his brief account of what was the first contact of
the Polos with the Tartar world, we recognize Marco's
characteristic trait, increasingly emphasized as the narrative proceeds, of intentionally, if discreetly, effacing or
attenuating the mention of the trade they practised, in
order to throw into relief the other and more noble
activities which they pursued among the Tartars. Thus,
he does not say that the two brothers *sold* to Berka the
jewels they had brought with them, but gives us to
understand that they offered them to the Khan, receiv-

ing from him in return double their value: whether in coins, in goods or on paper-money, is not known exactly. This is just the point we have to clarify.[3]

The ambiguity of Marco's expression is due to the more chivalrous rather than commercial phraseology used in this passage which describes the sovereign's reception of the two merchants and the business which they carried out. The intention is evidently to recall the attitude of friendly rivalry among equals in the exchange of liberalities and courtesies that took place between the powerful Khan and his guests. In reality, it stands to reason that this polite Oriental transaction has a positive commercial background which becomes visible behind Marco's veiled and ambiguous expressions as soon as the double value paid by Berka for the jewels is not interpreted merely as a euphemism but as a positive statement concerning a good bargain. In this case we have only to establish how the Khan did pay for the jewels he graciously accepted from the two Venetians.

Certainly the payment was not made in ready money because coins did not circulate at that time in that country. William of Rubruk tells us repeatedly that he was not able to buy anything with Byzantine gold and silver coins during his long journey across the same Russian and Western Asiatic borderlands.[4] The in-

---

[3] The Franco-Italian version (*Il Milione*, etc., Chap. III, p. 4) says: "Les deus frers li donnent toutes les joiaus qu'il avoient aportés. Et Barcha le prist mult volentiers et li pleient outre mesure. Il en fait leur doner bien deus tant que les joiaus ne valoient. Il les envoia a parer en plosor partie e furent mout bien parés." The last sentence is not very clear and has been suppressed by Yule-Cordier, *The Book*, etc., p. 4 and substituted after thorough discussion by a better version by Moule-Pelliot, *Description*, etc., p. 3, stating that the Polos were able to sell at a good profit in places in the neighborhood the things which Berka gave them in exchange for the jewels.

[4] Cf. *Sinica francisc.*, pp. 192, 3; 196, 4; 198, 11. "We could find

digenous population was suspicious of this sort of payment and "they rubbed the coins with their fingers, and put them to their noses to smell if they were copper." [5] Barter was general in those regions: in Russia on the basis of skins, and, in the Tartar borderlands, of linen or other tissues. The Mongolian *iascots*, used in Central and Eastern Asia, were lumps of bullion which represented a sort of monetary unity but were not usual tender for commercial intercourse.[6] Consequently it is not easy to find out how the business was transacted.

Some reliable old versions of Marco Polo's text confirm at this same point that the Khan did not pay the two merchants in money, but in goods, "which were well worth more than twice as much as the jewels were worth." [7] This circumstance seems to have prompted the Polos to remain in the country in order to sell the goods bartered for the jewels and to make money for their return home to Constantinople or Venice. This would be an excellent and almost authoritative explanation for the otherwise inexplicable decision of the Polo's to defer for a year or more the journey back to Europe and to settle down in the meantime in the dreary kingdom of Kipchak where nothing was produced that might have been attractive and valuable for an Occidental trader.

Considered from this angle, the magnanimity of

nothing to buy with gold and silver, but only with linen and other tissues, and those we had none." Rockhill, *The Journey*, etc., p. 88. In his *Pratica della Mercatura* (ed. A. Evans, Cambridge, Mass., 1937, p. 23), Francesco Balducci Pegolotti advises the merchants, en route from Genoa or Venice to China, to carry some bundles of most thin linen tissues which may be bartered when travelling through Persia.

[5] *Sinica francisc.*, p. 192.
[6] Rockhill, *The Journey*, etc., p. 156, n. 2.
[7] Cf. Marco Polo, *Description*, etc., p. 75 n. 1.

Berka appears to be one of the able tricks used by the
Tartar Khans, especially during this period, in order to
increase their stock of gold, precious stones and objects
of fixed value. A policy of this kind was then connected
with the gradual extension of paper-money throughout
the Mongolian empire. Friar William was only acquainted with Chinese paper-money, though since 1236
the Mongolians had adopted it on a smaller scale. While
it was introduced only during the last decades of that
country into Persia and other Western Asiatic countries,
with disastrous economic effects, yet it may be assumed
that Mongolian paper-money might have circulated
much earlier as legal currency throughout the empire,
including the regions where it had not yet been issued.[8]
At least Marco Polo explicitly affirms that the Grand
Khan caused it to be used in all the provinces, kingdoms
and lands subject to him, and asserts that all the peoples
over whom he ruled used it for their commerce. Many
times a year all those who had precious stones, pearls,
gold and silver were summoned to hand them over to
the mint where they were paid with money according to
the proper value. "And in this way"—Marco concludes—" the Grand Khan has all the gold and the
silver and the pearls and the precious stones of all his
lands." [9]

[8] Rockhill, *The Journey*, etc., p. 210 and Yule-Cordier's comment to
Marco Polo, *The Book*, etc., I, pp. 423-430.

[9] Marco Polo, *Description*, etc., p. 240; *The Book*, etc., I, p. 425; *Il
Milione*, etc., p. 92. This fact has been confirmed by Pegolotti more than
thirty years later (*La Pratica della Mercatura*, ed. A. Evans, p. 29),
with the explicit remark that the value of this paper currency was stable
and equivalent to the corresponding quantity of gold or silver. In reality,
it seems that Kubilai's policy successfully avoided the depreciation of this
paper money which, on the contrary, took place under his successors
and contributed to the overthrow of the Mongolian dynasty. Cf. A. T.
H. Charignon, *Le Livre de Marco Polo*, Peking, 1924, Vol. II, p. 106
et seq.

The chapter which he devotes to the Khan's "al-chemy," as he ironically calls it, contains some allusions to the policy of inflation based on the fluctuating value of this paper as compared with the increasing value of the merchandise. But the Venetian traveller also knows that this kind of forced currency was a great advantage for the economic life of the nomad populations extending through the whole continent, and a benefit to the merchants who could carry their money easily from the one end of the huge empire to the other as legal tender for investment in other merchandise. This paper-money represented the economic unity of the empire and at the same time the best way to overcome the primitive barter system which was entirely inadequate to the commercial, financial and political needs of this multifarious Asiatic commonwealth.

Now we can easily understand that Berka Khan was delighted, indeed, to obtain in such an unexpected way a lot of just those valuables that were so praised in his country and coveted more by his treasury than by his subjects. It is no wonder that he paid them twice as much as they were worth. But this payment was made either in goods which the Polo brothers could not carry away, or in a currency that they coud not spend outside of the Mongolian Empire. For the one reason or the other they were obliged to remain among the Nomads of the Volga-basin. It was only after a year of activity and experience in this borderland of Europe and Asia that they decided to set out for home.

But since war had broken out between Berka Khan and his cousin Hulagu, the conqueror of Persia, they were unable to turn westward, and so, leaving Bolgara, they went beyond the Volga at Ukek and proceded across the steppes to the east of the Caspian Sea directed toward Central Asia by the caravan route to the south of Lake Aral. From Marco's laconic report we gather only that the two travellers crossed a desert where "they found neither town nor village, falling in only with the tents of Tartars occupied with their cattle at pasture." [10] But we can draw some information about this journey from the report of Friar William of Rubruk who visited this borderland of the Golden Horde about ten years earlier in travelling from Ukek to Bolgara. We learn from his account that the traffic between the two principal towns of this extended region, called at that time the "Great Bulgaria," was carried in boats on the Volga river. The Friar was surprised and shocked by the unsuspected fact that the whole region was inhabited by Saracens "professing stronger the law of Mahommed than any other nation." [11] In the decade between the two travels no essential changes had come to pass in this region. What had been for the Friar an object of scandal happended to be beneficial for the two traders. For the first time they had an opportunity to live among the Moslems and to become familiar with the customs and manners of Mohammedan tribes among whom they later had to spend three years during their stay in Central Asia.

Crossing the steppes of Western Siberia they reached Bokhara, the capital of Western Turkestan, where they

[10] Marco Polo, *Description*, etc., p. 76; *The Book*, etc., I, p. 4.

[11] Rockhill, *The Journey*, etc., p. 120 *et seq.* and the more extended description of this region by Yule-Cordier in Marco Polo, *The Book*, etc., I, p. 5 *et seq.* For the political and ethonological situation in this country, cf. C. Gérard, *Les Bulgares de la Volga et les Slaves du Danube*, Paris, 1939, reviewed by A. Vasiliev in the *American Historical Review*, Vol. XLVI, 1941, p. 118. A short introduction on "Trade and Communication in Eastern Europe A. D. 800-1200" by A. Meyendorff in *Travel and Traders of the Middle Ages*, ed. by A. P. Newton, New York, 1930, p. 104 *et seq.* Passages from Arabic travellers and geographers concerning the regions of Bolgara and Sarai in Hennig's *Terrae Incognitae*, II, p. 220 *et seq.*

passed three years with all the ways back to the West
blocked by the war. We are not informed about their
activity in this rich and commercial town, but it is
possible to recognize the influence of this long stay on
the further exploration of the Asiatic continent. In
fact, the three years spent by the Polos in this flourishing country furnished the essential conditions for the
success of both their journeys across Asia and the best
preparation for the later exploits of Marco, in spite of
the fact that he did not visit this region.

With the neighboring city of Samarkand, Bokhara
was at that epoch the most important commercial center
of continental Asia, especially with regard to the transit-
trade from China, Persia, Afghanistan and India. In
the bazars and warehouses of these places the traders
of all these countries met incessantly. The important
local industries were in the hands of the permanent
population which included very considerable and busy
groups of Moslems, Nestorians and Jews. The rulers of
the region were at that time the Tartar princes of
Central Asia belonging to the dynasty of Genghis Khan.
Besides the indigenous Turkish dialect, many languages
were spoken in the cities and markets of this vast borderland. But Persian was preferred in the local commercial intercourse of foreign traders as well as in the
intercontinental trade relations between the Black Sea
and Peking. Marco Polo considered Western Turkestan
as a Persian province.[12] It was certainly in this place
that the two Venetians learned this language, just as
they had become acquainted with the leading Mongolian and Turkish languages during their travels in
the kingdom of Kipchak. Marco learned from them on

---

[12] Marco Polo, *The Book*, etc., I, p. 10 and Yule's comment to this
passage and to the description of Samarkand, *loc. cit.*, p. 186.

their way from Venice to Asia the official Mongolian and the commercial Persian language which were usually spoken in the Polo family as fluently as their native Venetian dialect.[13] There was a great and active Persian colony at Khanbaliq during the reign of Kubilai Khan.[14]

Thus Marco was well prepared for his own experiences and for a quick and direct understanding of the characteristic aspects of Asiatic life. But it was evident at the same time that this particular education of the young traveller accustomed him to consider and to depict the peoples and manners of the whole continent from a Tartar angle and with a Persian touch. For that reason he shows less comprehension and less realistic discernment in his relations with the peoples of Asia living outside this cultural and linguistic sphere. This Central-Asiatic initiation of his father and uncle was decisive for young Marco, and it prevented him from adapting his mind to the national character of the Chinese people, and from overcoming an unmistakable

---

[13] For the languages spoken in Mongol Court and administration, cf. *ibid.*, pp. 27-30. For Persian applied to the languages of foreigners at the Mongol Court, *ibid.*, p. 380 n. and Vol. II, p. 5 n. Many short hints to the languages used at Karakorum may be found in the reports of the missionaries, *Sinica francisc., passim.*

[14] Cf. A. C. Moule, *Christians in China*, etc., *passim*. For the Chinese intercourse with Persia see Yule-Cordier, *Cathay*, etc., I, p. 92 *et seq.* Persian was spoken by the Moslems in the region east of Lake Balkash, formerly inhabited by the Karakitai, "a very long way off from Persia" (cf. Rockhill, *The Journey*, etc., p. 139 *et seq.*). For the diffusion of the Persian language in Central and Eastern Asia, cf. the note of H. Cordier in the *Addenda* to Yule's edition of *The Book of Marco Polo*, etc., 1923, p. 71. Friar Paschal of Vitoria affirms in his letter written at Almaligh on St. Lawrence Day, 1338, that the Coman language and Uigur characters were used in his days "throughout all the kingdoms and empires of the Tartars, Persians, Chaldeans, Medes and Kathay" (cf. *Sinica francisc.*, I, p. 503). On this international Asiatic, commercial and official language, cf. P. Pelliot "A propos des Comans," *Journal Asiatique*, 1920, p. 115 *et seq.*

Islamic influence in his description of India. The Tartar, Persian, and Arabic nomenclature of his book lead us to suppose that he always preferred to join the colonies and communities whose languages had been familiar to him from adolescence through his daily routine and from intercourse with the elder Polos.

He obviously obtained from them the data for his description of Samarkand, a city he never visited and which was at all times no less important than Bokhara as an historic and commercial center.[15] In such a way he was able to trace the political conditions of the region and to retell the local legend of the "Wonder of the Pillar," going back to the alleged conversion to Christianity of Chagatai, son of Genghis Khan and first Tartar ruler of Central Asia. This information is scanty and vague enough, but it is the first contribution to knowledge about a country of which the Western world had not received any direct information since the time of Alexander the Great.

* * *

After three years spent by the Venetian travellers in that region, without having found any possibility of returning to the West, it happened that an envoy of Kubilai Khan sent to Hulagu, the conqueror and ruler of Persia, arrived at Bokhara on his way back to " the lord of all the Tartars in the world." [16] This envoy proposed to the Polos to follow him to the court of the Grand Khan, as neither Kubilai nor he himself had, until then, ever seen any Latins, in spite of a keen desire on their part to became acquainted with some of them.

This detail, though of negative value, is interesting and may be indirectly confirmed. Kubilai had spent

[15] Marco Polo, *The Book*, etc., I, p. 183 *et seq.*
[16] Marco Polo, *The Book*, etc., I, p. 10.

almost all his life in the eastern parts of the vast Mongolian empire, and from his youth his policy and culture had been influenced by the Chinese surroundings in which he lived. It is probable that his visits to Karakorum, the capital, were rare and brief, so that it can be affirmed without doubt that he really never met people from Western Europe. Mangu Khan, his brother and predecessor, Batu, Sartach and other Genghis-khanid princes, had not been entirely cut off from the Latin world, although they had derived little advantage from their rare and fleeting personal contacts with envoys and individuals from the West.

In any case even high dignitaries of the Mongolian courts had a very vague and inaccurate conception of Western Europe. The Tartar nobleman who accompanied William of Rubruk as an envoy of Batu to the court of the emperor at Karakorum told the Friar that a report had gone the rounds among the Mongols that the Pope was five hundred years old.[17] Furthermore he asked the friar if in his country there were sheep, oxen and horses. Evidently the horizons of this Tartar dignitary were not very extended. If we consider that he was the son of a high officer of Batu's army, we may infer that the great incursion of his hordes into Hungary up to the gates of Italy contributed but little to a more correct conception of the Western world among the Mongols. The Chinese knew even less about such matters. Consequently Kubilai's envoy was perfectly well informed about the ignorance of his sovereign. All these circumstances contribute to our understanding of the exceptional task that awaited the Polos at the court of the most powerful monarch of their time. The historical importance of their unanticipated mission de-

---

[17] Rockhill, *The Journey*, etc., p. 133.

pends upon the fact that they were the first direct and reliable informants capable of giving the emperor a picture of the western European civilisation.

Lured by promises of an honorable and liberal reception, as well as of a comfortable and safe journey, the two brothers set out together, directed their steps " eastward and northward " with the envoys of the Grand Khan, and made their way across regions which Marco Polo was later on to see and to describe. They arrived after one year at the court of Kubilai. Just where this court was at that time Marco does not say. When he ascended the throne, the Khan's residence was in the vicinity of the Great Wall, probably in a horde of tents after the Mongolian fashion, recalling the nomad life of his ancestors. Soon afterwards he took up his abode at Shang-tu, a place nearly 350 miles to the north of Peking; later on this remained his favorite summer seat. In 1264, *i. e.* shortly before the arrival of the two Venetians, Kubilai transferred his capital to Peking, which, in the official language, was called by its Turkish appellation of Khanbaliq, the Khan's city. Under this name this newest and latest metropolis of the Mongolian empire was known to Europe through the accounts of Marco and of the Franciscan missionaries of the fourteenth century.[18]

We are unable to determine whether Maffeo and Niccolò went this far on their first journey, but at all

[18] Marco Polo's description of the city in *The Book.* etc., I, p. 374 *et seq.*; for the summer palace of Shang-tu, *ibid.*, p. 304 *et seq.* The very poor details contained in the reports of the missionaries concern almost exclusively the churches and the Christian population of the Capital. Cf. *Sinica francisc.*, I, p. 602. The most detailed description after that of Marco Polo is contained in the report of Odorico da Pordenone, *ibid.*, p. 471 *et seq.* The second time the Polo brothers, accompanied by Marco, first stopped at the Khan's summer palace of Shang-tu, then called Kemanfu (*The Book*, etc., I, p. 25).

events it is certain that they were the first Europeans, within the memory of man, who crossed the boundaries of Chinese territory. It is probable that, after their inconclusive stay at Bokhara, their decision to proceed so far was motivated more by curiosity and the spirit of adventure than by the desire to seek new markets and commercial outlets. In the meantime they had effectually transformed their status of merchants into that of guests and informants of the Grand Khan. By winning his confidence they were able to ascend still higher in the social scale and to attain the position they finally reached, together with the young Marco: that of the counsellors and functionaries of that great sovereign. Let us follow with a critical eye the stages of their brilliant and extraordinary career as described in a much too laconic style and with few and poor details in the prologue of Marco's book.

The prologue relates at this point that Kubilai desired the Venetians to inform him regarding the Emperor (probably Baldwin, Latin emperor of Byzantium), of his dignity, justice and military power and of those of other Christian states; of the Pope, the Church, and of all the customs of the Latins. Kubilai must have been all the more pleased with the information he received in as much as the Polo brothers gave it to him in his own Tartar tongue, which they had mastered in the course of their journeys. The confidence which they must have inspired in the monarch was such that, after several months of residence at his court, he despatched the Polos on a mission to the Pope, providing them with the " Golden Tablet," reserved for his special emissaries, at the sight of which every functionary was to do homage and obeisance. Probably this mission was suggested to the Khan by the Polo brothers themselves, who only by such means could hope to return safe and sound to their homes. Bearers of those tablets were considered inviolate all over the empire. It was thanks to this safe-conduct that they actually succeeded, after three years of travel, in reaching Laias, on the shores of the Mediterranean, leaving far behind them the Tartar dignitary who had been charged by Kubilai to accompany them to Rome.[19] And now we see the two Venetians who had left their warehouse at Soldaia with a handful of jewels, returning to the West as ambassadors from the Grand Khan, and being treated throughout the immense empire for the duration of their journey with all the deference due such exalted dignity.

* * *

The mission entrusted to the two brothers had no political design. They must have given Kubilai Khan such an enthusiastic and eloquent picture of Occidental civilisation as to induce him to send to the Pope an embassy of a purely cultural and religious nature. Marco clearly reports that the Emperor sent letters to the Pontiff and at the same time gave his envoys oral instructions concerning his personal wishes and interests. None of those letters is preserved, but the double form of this commission reveals the merely courteous tenor of the written message and the unpolitical character of the whole mission. Since the Pontiffs and the sovereigns of Europe were wont to receive from the Tartar rulers only insolent and provocative letters, these of Kubilai might have represented a pleasant and encouraging exception.

Kubilai requested the Pontiff to send him as many as a hundred intelligent men devoted to the Christian faith

[19] This " Baron," whose name was Cogatal, certainly a high dignitary of Kubilai's court, fell sick on the way and was left behind by the Polos. Cf. *The Book*, etc., I, pp. 13 and 15.

7

and acquainted with the Seven Arts, who " should know well how to argue and to show plainly to the idolaters and to all the classes of the people that all their laws were quite different from those of the Christians, and how all the idols which they keep in their houses and worship are things of the devil, and who should know how to prove clearly by reason that the Christian religion was better than theirs." [20] Besides, the two brothers were charged to bring to the Tartar court some oil from the lamp that burned before the Holy Sepulchre in Jerusalem.

These requests have always aroused some surprise, and it has been easy to doubt or deny them. Kubilai, who was publicly known to be an adherent of Buddhism, nevertheless exercised towards many religions of his empire that superstitious and condescending tolerance traditional among the Genghiskhanides rulers of whatever faith. As to the oil from the sacred lamp, it may be admitted that it was desired by the Christian entourage of the Grand Khan, and especially by the women of his family and court. It is even probable that this oil was intended for practises of magic rather than as an object of devotion, since the Nestorians did not know the use of holy oil in their ritual while on the other hand they had accepted for centuries the influence of Asiatic Shamanism and all its practice of incantation and sorcery.[21] Friar William observed that the Nestorian priests of Karakorum used to dip their bread into a mixture composed of some oil " that they called holy "

[20] Marco Polo, *Description*, etc., p. 79; *The Book*, etc., I, p. 13. As it is known the Seven, or Liberal Arts include Rhetoric, Logic, and Grammar (i. e. Latin) as a *Trivium*, and the *Quadrivium* of Arithmetic, Astronomy, Music and Geometry.

[21] For the Nestorian use of oil, cf. Rockhill, *The Journey*, etc., p. 105, n. 2. Many examples of magical practice are described by the missionaries, e. g. *Sinica francisc.*, p. 265 *et seq.*, 285, 303 etc.

and an ointment with which Mary Magdalene "had anointed the feet of our Lord." [22] The same oil served for the making of the consecrated bread which they divided in some circumstances among those present in their church.

Be that as it may, to give its rightful value to the request of the oil on the part of Kubilai it is sufficient to recall the fact that Marco Polo was present in 1284 when the special ambassadors, who had been sent to Ceylon for the purpose, arrived at the court of the Grand Khan with extraordinary pomp and solemnity reverently bearing with them a bowl, some hair and two teeth of Buddha. "Then the great Kaan commands that all the people both regulars and others should go to meet those relics which they were made to understand that they were of Adam." [23] The magic power of the bowl was said to increase fivefold the food put into it.

As to the requests addressed to the Pope in regard to the propagation of Christian doctrines in his lands, these without doubt were misinterpreted if not intentionally altered by the Polo brothers, in order to increase the importance of their mission and to add greater lustre to their name. But their exaggerations and pride have a concrete and psychological foundation upon which light can be thrown. The problem must be carefully studied and considered within the general framework of contemporary opinions and experiences.

[22] *Ibid.*, p. 214, 280, respectively.
[23] Marco Polo, *Description*, etc., p. 411; *The Book*, etc., II, p. 320. The Saracens of Ceylon, as narrated by Marco Polo in the same chapter, say that the teeth, the hair, and the dish were those of Adam. Adam's Peak in Ceylon has been for ages a place of pilgrimage to Buddhist, Hindu and Mahometan (Yule, *loc. cit.*, n. 5). Keeping his usual neutrality toward the different creeds, Kubilai probably gave in this way a satisfaction to the numerous Moslems living at Khanbaliq, and to the Nestorians, too.

It may be maintained beyond doubt that Kubilai never asserted that the " law " of his people was all the work of the devil. Neither a Mongolian Shamanist nor a Chinese Buddhist would have designated their religious rites and magic practices as " devilish things." This conviction and its very expression are both characteristically Christian: these words are used with peculiar frequency by the missionaries, either to condemn the practices of magic common among the Orientals, or to render particularly abominable those aspects of Asiatic religions which appeared to them to have something in common with Christianity.

The Polo brothers returning to the West with these impressions and placing in such clear relief the Kubilai's pretended preferences for Christianity confirmed and encouraged the age-long belief in an illusion which even the experiences and admonitions of the last missionaries had not succeeded in dispelling. In fact, it is probable that this widespread conviction had accompanied the brothers even to the court of the Grand Khan, predisposing them to misunderstand the religious rites and the political designs of the sovereign.

The origin of the misunderstandings and the true intentions of Kubilai are revealed to us from a passage in an edition of the *Milione* which Ramusio had before him and inserted in his publication of Marco Polo's text.[24] Messer Marco therein relates how, on their first visit to the court of the Grand Khan, the Polo brothers were much amazed to see that Kubilai had not yet decided to be baptized although he honored the Christian religion and allowed incense to be burned before

[24] The whole passage is reproduced in Marco Polo's *Description*, etc., p. 202, in Yule's note to *The Book*, etc., I, p. 348 (Chap. VI) and by A. C. Moule, *Christians in China*, p. 135.

him by the Nestorian priests, and on the feasts of Easter and Christmas devoutly kissed their Gospels.

As Kubilai " does the like at the principal feasts of the Saracens, Jews and idolaters " these practices appear to be purely external and superstitious. It might also be supposed that the emperor, being the son of a Nestorian mother, may have had a preference for Christianity, at least in a particular interpretation of that sect. Whether and to what extent his sentiments were attracted toward Christian doctrines and morals can be indirectly established through his reply to the Venetians who had dared to solicit his conversion. Let us listen to his own words, as reported by Marco Polo:

He said to them: How do you wish me to make myself a Christian? You see that the Christians who are in these parts are totally ignorant so that they do nothing and have no power; and you see that these idolaters do whatever they wish, and when I sit at table the cups which are in the middle of the hall come to me full of wine or drink or of other things without anyone touching them, and I drink with them. They compel storms to go in whatever direction they please, and do many wonderful things, and as you know their idols speak and foretell them all that they wish. But if I am converted to the faith of Christ and am made a Christian, then my barons and other people who are not attached to the faith of Christ would say to me: What reason has moved you to baptism, and to hold the faith of Christ? What virtues or what miracles have you seen of him? And these idolaters say that what they do they do it by the holiness and virtue of the idols. Then I shall not know what to answer them so that there will be a great error between them and these idolaters who do such things with their arts and sciences; and they will easily be able to make me die.

As can be seen from the monarch's confessions, he

considers religion merely an instrument of his power and, quite neglecting the moral worth and doctrinal content of each faith, he judges of their excellence in proportion to the magical power of their priests. While the Christians do not practice the art of necromancy, the Lamas and Shamans are capable, instead, of making objects invisibly change their position, of inducing or driving away bad weather, of predicting the future, and of doing wonderful things. The Franciscan missionaries and Marco Polo himself repeatedly described the incantations practised by these exorcisers and soothsayers towards whom Kubilai continued to show the same devout respect that they had enjoyed from his predecessors.[25]

We can see from this how, with all his attachment to Buddhism, with his respect for Nestorian Christianity, his interest in Catholicism and his wise tolerance of all other religions, Kubilai remained at heart a convinced Shamanist, attached to that rough and primitive Mongolian tradition which confirmed the practices of witchcraft as being useful and just. The Polos were right in considering these exorcisms, sorceries and incantations as diabolic work in open contradiction with the Christian faith, and they proposed to refute them with the approval of the Khan, whose intention evidently was to ask the Pope for men equally as clever in the arts and sciences as they were, and as capable not only of competing with his soothsayers in their practices of magic, but also of surpassing them in the fields of practical activity. He was probably thinking of that mechanical skill of the Westerners, in the person

---

[25] As the examples are too numerous for quotation and discussion cf. *Sinica francisc.*, p. 605, art. " divinators " and the Index to Yule-Cordier's edition of Marco Polo, *The Book*, etc.

of the Parisian goldsmith, which had met with so much approval at the court of this brother Mangu Khan.[26]

In his palaces at Shang-tu and Peking there were some imitations of the complicated automatic fountains admired and described by William of Rubruk as an extraordinary technical achievement performed by the French artist. Kubilai certainly had still in mind the beautiful throne made by Cosmas, the Ruthenian goldsmith whom Küyük Khan greatly cherished because of his workmanship and artistic dexterity. Since that time the Tartar court was populated with Ruthenians and Hungarians " scientes Latinum et Gallicum." [27] Mangu Khan transferred a troop of German slaves to the mines of Tsungaria where they had to extract metals and manufacture weapons.[28] It was a Nestorian Christian from an unidentified country of the Near-East to whom Kubilai entrusted in 1263 the offices of Western astronomy and of medicine.[29]

It can be deduced from all these facts that the Tartar rulers were traditionally wont to associate the idea of Western Christianity with that of art, science and technical skill. The Polo brothers were not aware of this particular interpretation of Christian civilization which still prevails among the peoples of Asia. They rendered truthfully Kubilai's mind and intention when they associated the teaching of the Seven Arts with the

[26] Cf. *supra*, p. 53 and n. 42, and for the imitations of this contrivance in China, cf. Rockhill, *The Journey*, etc., p. 208, n. 2.

[27] *Sinica francisc.*, p. 217. For more details about these contrivances and the history of Western influence on the Mongolian court cf. the Author's *Storia Letteraria delle Scoperte Geografiche*, Firenze, 1937, pp. 73-104.

[28] *Ibid.*, p. 225 and Rockhill, *op. cit.*, p. 136 *et seq.*

[29] A. C. Moule, *Christians in China*, p. 228 *et seq.* The activity of the Polos as builders of mangonels at the siege of Saianfu may be recalled here (cf. *supra*, p. 54).

preaching of the Christian doctrine. While the Nestorians living in the Far East were incapable of doing anything of this kind, the Christians of the West represented with their liberal arts and mechanical skill the
rational power of intellect contrasting with the magic
jugglery of Oriental religions and abilities. It was the
emperor's intention to join these two different intellectual tendencies for the increase of his political power
and personal prestige.

For him as for the Polo brothers, art, science and
culture were strictly connected with religious faith and
priestly dignity, both considered the spiritual background of human achievements. Asking for men especially versed in theological matters Kubilai expected that
they should have the power of working " miracles " in
a different way from that of conjuring demons and wor-
shipping idols. For the administration of the empire the
Grand Khan needed foreigners as advisers, officials and
agents. His Monogolian countrymen were unequal to
the task because of their cultural insufficiency and the
lack of political traditions. On the other hand, the
Chinese mandarinate was reluctant to cooperate with
the conqueror. One hundred skilled and learned men
from Europe would have been a great help to the
ambitious sovereign.

As the shrewd Oriental he was, he made the two
Venetians believe that his conversion might depend
upon the success of the Christian mission he required
from the Roman Pontiff. This was the sort of price he
vaguely held out to his envoys, and consequently, to
the Pope himself, if they were to hope for his conversion.
In the same way his predecessors and vassals had always
had recourse to similar flattery whenever they wanted
to secure for themselves the assistance of the Christians

or the advantages of their friendship. This time, Kubilai lured, through the same means, experts in the *Quadrivium* of the arts and sciences, men who could be useful to him in putting into effect the vast projects and the great undertakings which made his long reign illustrious and a benefit to the country.

Deeming himself a god upon earth, he considered the supernatural as an instrument of his will and power and, being spiritually limited, he could appreciate only the practical and utilitarian aspects of all religions. This fact the Polos were unable to understand, and they doubtless returned westward convinced that they were fulfilling a mission for the faith which would redound to the glory of Christianity. We know no other merchants then associated with the missionaries in this work of propaganda, in the task of bringing the Far East near to Catholicism and to Latin civilization. But, just as at the present time, every respectable merchant away from his own country considers himself almost as its representative and holds himself morally obligated to win for it not only commercial outlets, but also friends, interest and esteem, so it was then, in an era of intensive propagation of the faith, that every Christian who happened to be among the pagans considered himself as a messenger of truth, and felt that such action on his part would redound, not only to his material profits, but also to the attainment of worldly glory and the salvation of his soul in heaven.[30]

Harbouring these sentiments, the two Venetians proceeded upon their homeward journey. It took them three years to cross Asia before they reached Accon in

[30] Samuel Eliot Morison affirms in his *Life of Christopher Columbus*, Boston, 1942, Vol. I, p. 217, n. 9. that this missionary motive lasted for centuries in the reports of colonial enterprises. " To read the charter of the Massachusetts Bay Company of 1629, one would suppose that the unique object of the Puritan fathers was to convert the natives."

the month of April 1269. There they learned that the
Pope had died, whereupon they decided to await at
Venice the election of his successor. When, after another
three and a half years of travelling, they returned to
the court of the Grand Khan, they presented to him
the young Marco instead of the hundred doctors he had
asked for. The two learned friars who had been chosen
by the Pope to accompany them had stopped along the
route.[31] More than two hundred years later, Christopher
Columbus began the *Journal* of his first transatlantic
voyage with a discreet disapproval of the Pope's failure
to send to China the " doctors " requested by the Grand
Khan for the conversion of the subjects.[32] The Admiral
considered his own undertaking to be the fulfillment of
Kubilai's desire, although his caravels did not carry
priests or missionaries in the first attempt to reach the
fabulous lands described by Marco Polo.

Thus young Marco had come from Venice with no
other preparation than that of his intelligence, and no
further experience than that of his teens. His father
and his uncle, almost Orientals themselves, had prepared him to live and move about in that Eastern world.
More than his precursors, they had become his masters
and outriders. They placed him, as he was, without the
apanage of the liberal arts or the ecclesiastical habit,
in the service of Kubilai, who thrust upon him, during
the course of seventeen years, as many forms of em-
ployment as a hundred masters of the *Trivium* and
the *Quadrivium* would not have had the capacity to
discharge with as much success.

[31] The names of the two Dominican friars—Nicolas of Vicenza and
William of Tripolis—are mentioned by Marco Polo, *The Book*, etc., I,
p. 22. The new Pope, Gregory X, did not entrust to the Polos his reply
to Kubilai, but to the friars, to whom the Pontiff gave proper credentials
and broad ecclesiastical authority. These Preaching friars were too
frightened to proceed and turned back as soon as they got to Laias.

[32] S. E. Morison, *loc. cit.*

ABBREVIATIONS USED IN FOOTNOTES

Ch. V. Langlois. Ch. V. Langlois, *La Connaissance de la Nature et du Monde au Moyen Age d'après quelques écrits français à l'usage des laïcs* (Paris, 1911).

Marco Polo, *Il Milione*. Marco Polo, *Il Milione*. Prima edizione integrale a cura di L. Foscolo Benedetto (Firenze, 1928).

Marco Polo. *The Book* etc. *The Book of Ser Marco Polo the Venetian concerning the kingdoms and marvels of the East*. Translated and edited with notes, by Col. Sir Henry Yule, 3rd edition revised by H. Cordier (2 vols., London, New York, 1927).

Marco Polo, *Description, etc.* Marco Polo, *The Description of the World*, ed. by A. C. Moule & P. Pelliot (2 vols. London, 1938) containing: Vol. I the English translation; Vol. II A transcription of Z, the Latin codex in the Cathedral Library at Toledo.

Ramusio. G. B. Ramusio, *Secondo Volume delle Navigationi & Viaggi nel quale si contengono l'Historia delle cose de' Tartari* etc. *descritte da Marco Polo gentilhuomo venetiano* etc. (Venetia, 1559).

Rockhill etc. *The Journey of William of Rubruck to the Eastern parts of the World* etc. ed. by William W. Rockhill (London, Hakluyt Society, 1900).

Sinica Franciscana. Anastasius van den Wyngaert, *Sinica Franciscana*, Vol. I: Itinera et Relationes Fratrum Minorum saec. XIII et XIV. (Quaracchi-Firenze, 1929).

J. K. Wright. John Kirtland Wright, *The Geographical Lore of the Time of the Crusades etc.* (New York, Amer. Geograph. Society, 1925).

Yule-Cordier, *Cathay* etc. Sir H. Yule, *Cathay and the Way Thither* etc. New edition by H. Cordier (4 vols. London, Hakluyt Society 1913-1916).

Zarncke. " Der Presbyter Johannes " in *Abhandlungen der kgl. Sächsischen Gesellschaft der Wissenschaften*, Leipzig 1876 and 1879.

95

INDEX *

---

* Since this book is not especially intended for Orientalists, Asiatic names are not given in phonetical transcription but in the forms used by mediaeval authors and in most of the modern translations of their works.

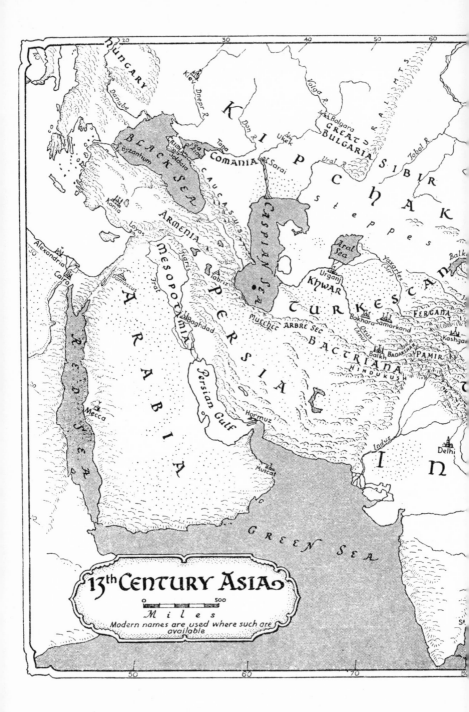

13th CENTURY ASIA

0   500
Miles
Modern names are used where such are available

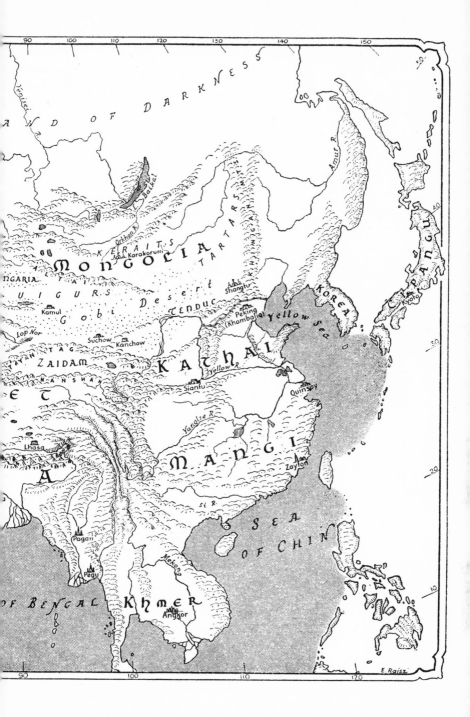